deep dark
CHOCOLATE

D1412602

deep dark CHOCOLATE

DECADENT RECIPES
for the serious
CHOCOLATE LOVER

by
SARA PERRY

photographs by
FRANCE RUFFENACH

CHRONICLE BOOKS
SAN FRANCISCO

Library of Congress Cataloging-in-Publication Data available.
ISBN: 978-0-8118-6089-5
Manufactured in China

Designed by Sara Schneider
Food styling by Elisabet der Nederlanden
Prop styling by Spork
Typesetting by Janis Reed

The photography team thanks The Gardener for generously sharing their beautiful merchandise with us as props throughout the book.
The Gardener, 1836 Fourth St., Berkeley, California
www.thegardener.com.

www.saraperry.com
www.deepdarkchocolatebook.com

10 9 8 7 6 5 4 3 2 1

Chronicle Books
680 Second Street
San Francisco, California 94107
www.chroniclebooks.com

dedication and acknowledgments

To my friends and colleagues Amy Treadwell, Jane Zwinger, Kathlyn Meskel, and Karen Brooks. Your support, insights, and ways around the kitchen (and a paragraph) make me shine.

Thanks go to the many chefs and cooks I have interviewed over the years for my weekly Oregonian column, especially Jim Roberts, Jeanne Subotnick, Christopher Israel, Lisa Allen, Dominique Guelin, Gerry Frank, Evelyn Franz, Ken Forkish, Wednesday Wild, Aubrey Lindley, and Jesse Manis. Also to those friends and colleagues who generously shared their ideas, expertise, time, and recipes, especially Martha Holmberg, Matthew Meskel, Kieran Murphy, and Kristi and Chris Preston. To Karen Kirtley, for her excellent work on the early stages of this manuscript, and to copy editor Carrie Bradley for her suggestions and attention to detail. Thanks, Carrie. A special thanks goes to Frankie Whitman of Scharffen Berger Chocolate Makers for generous provisions of chocolate for testing. And, as always, my deepest thanks go to Bill LeBlond, senior editor at Chronicle Books, for his friendship, his great ideas, and the opportunity to do what I love.

TABLE *of* CONTENTS

chocolate, anyone•

C'mon in. Yes, *you*. This is the place—and the book—to indulge those deep, dark chocolate dreams of the perfect fudge sauce, a big ol' chocolate cake piled high with thick, rich frosting, and a luscious, deep, dark chocolate ice cream. What's even better is that you can make them all by yourself for fun, work, a romantic dinner, your next wedding (hey, these are modern times)—or, go ahead, make one just for yourself.

Dark chocolate is more than the quintessential comfort food. It is the new coffee: an affordable daily luxury with its own menu of intensities, flavors, and special infusions. Like fine wines, too, premium dark chocolates have distinctive characteristics. The artful labels that catch your eye are helpful guides to the origin of the cocoa beans, the cocoa-solids percentage, and the chocolate's particular flavor profile. If you're confused by words such as "cacao" and *"criollo"* or by percentages that resemble grades on a homework assignment, the "Know Your Chocolate" section (page 11) is here to help you understand the terms. Recipe by recipe, *Deep Dark Chocolate* helps you choose the best dark chocolates for baking, cooking, and eating out of hand.

If you plan your day right, you can kick it off with Hot Chocolate Waffles with Chocolate-Hazelnut Spread (page 157), then look forward to a mid-morning break with a slice of One-Bite-to-Heaven Chocolate

Yeast Cake (page 72) or a Chocolate Dream Scone with Mascarpone Spread (page 154). To top it off, I wouldn't refuse a nice chunk of Bittersweet Caramel Honeycomb (page 178) or an espresso cup steaming with European-Style Drinking Chocolate (page 184).

As for chocolate cookies, snacks, and bittersweet candies, consider these words attributed to seventeenth-century French aristocrat Madame de Sévigné: "If you are not feeling well, if you have not slept, chocolate will revive you. But you have no chocolate! My dear, how will you ever manage?" All the more reason to double the batch of Chocolate Cookies with All the Chips (page 37) and to pass around a plateful of Good Ol' Fudgy Brownies (page 55).

You're right to assume no birthday could be properly celebrated without a fabulous dark chocolate birthday cake, four layers high with *two* kinds of chocolate frosting and candleholders made of—you guessed it—dark chocolate truffles or fudge. Your kids will delight over Some More S'more Pie, Please (page 95), and Full-Tilt Dark Chocolate with Zabaglione (page 119) will have dinner guests asking for more (as well as asking for the recipe).

Dark-chocolate lovers have always known that their favorite food adds shadowy richness, earthy fragrance, and elegant nuance to show-stopping desserts as well as everyday comfort food. Dark chocolate goes to the essence of what chocolate *is* because dark chocolate has a wealth of cocoa solids, and these give chocolate its flavor and color. Dark chocolate also contains cocoa butter, which carries that wonderful flavor to our taste buds and makes it linger. As a bonus, premium dark chocolate has mystery. It's intense and snappy. Brilliantly fruity. Slightly tart. Have no doubt about it, chocolate is habit-forming.

Once you've bought the best dark chocolate you can find, take it home, taste it, and try any of the recipes in this book. You'll know then (as if you didn't know already) why deep, dark chocolate is irresistible.

KNOW YOUR

chocolate

Chocolate as we know it today is a far cry from the cold, peppery drink the Aztec Emperor Montezuma handed to Cortez in 1519. This was sweet revenge. This was a divine potion to celebrate the second coming of Quetzalcoatl, the fair-skinned Aztec god of wisdom, knowledge, and chocolate.

For centuries, chocolate was primarily enjoyed as a beverage. Its properties were legendary. Montezuma drank a goblet as an aphrodisiac; Casanova preferred it to champagne; and Brillat-Savarin, the famous nineteenth-century French jurist, writer, and gastronome, used it as a mild tranquilizer in his later years. It's been no secret that chocolate is a provocative and addictive flavor. Today, thanks to the ingenuity and skill of generations of chocolate makers, there are countless ways to enjoy it and scores of chocolates from which to choose.

Let's begin by exploring the varieties of dark chocolate we can use to create recipes every bit as seductive as their essential ingredient. We who love deep, dark chocolate are a devoted group, showing bias for the bittersweet and the essence of chocolate itself.

VARIETIES OF DARK CHOCOLATE

Here are some short-and-sweet explanations of chocolate in its many favorite forms:

unsweetened chocolate

Also known as *chocolate liquor*, *baking chocolate*, or *bitter chocolate*, unsweetened chocolate is simply cacao beans ground to a smooth paste with no added sugar or fat. It consists of two components: cocoa solids (the solids are what give chocolate its color and flavor) and cocoa butter (the butter is what makes the chocolate melt in your mouth and the flavor linger).

dark chocolate

This term defines both bittersweet and semisweet chocolate. If you're curious about the significance of that percentage sign on the label of your dark, bittersweet, or semisweet chocolate bar, consult "Chocolate Terminology" (page 16). As you'll see, the higher the percentage of chocolate liquor, the stronger the chocolate flavor will be. Will those percentages interfere with how a recipe turns out? Will a 60 percent chocolate give the same results as a 68 percent or a 70 percent? For the recipes in this book, the answer is, "Yes." There are exceptions, where I request a particular percentage—for example, in Deep, Dark Chocolate Ice Cream (page 134) the recipe calls for 3 1/2 ounces premium dark chocolate (no higher than 62 percent). That's because the higher the percentage, the more cocoa butter is present. And since cocoa butter freezes harder than butterfat, it makes the ice cream harder to eat (it also can become grainy).

As the percentage of chocolate liquor increases, the chocolate becomes less sweet and the amount of cocoa butter (that is, fat) increases as well. The recipes in *Deep Dark Chocolate* allow for a range up to and including 72 percent. Just remember, the higher the percentage, the more chocolate flavor and the less sugar will be present.

bittersweet and semisweet chocolate

These dark chocolates are the heart and soul of this book, but you won't find their names in the lists of ingredients (although you will see "bittersweet" to describe the taste). That's because the terms are becoming outmoded. They are not standardized, so one brand's bittersweet can be another brand's semisweet. Because neither one contains milk, when it comes to recipes (or to our taste buds), the two are interchangeable.

semisweet and bittersweet chocolate chips and

Chocolate chips and morsels are specially formulated to tolerate high heat and contact with hot baking sheets without melting or scorching. That's good when it comes to your favorite cookie, but may not be so good if you substitute the chips for baking chocolate. They don't melt like other dark chocolates because they contain less cocoa butter. While I often (if chocolate chunks were good enough for Ruth Wakefield to use when she created the first chocolate chip cookie in 1937, they're good enough for me), I stay away from substituting melted chocolate chips for melted baking chocolate.

dark chocolate buttons

These chocolate wafers are about the size of nickels. They react the same way bar or solid chocolate would in a recipe, but save you the trouble of chopping. (Unlike chips or morsels, they are not formulated to tolerate high heat by removing some of the cocoa butter.) They are sometimes sold as pastilles.

unsweetened cocoa powder

This superfine powder is pulverized chocolate liquor with much of the fat (cocoa butter) pressed out, making it a low-fat chocolate ingredient. Its percentage of cocoa butter varies from 10 to 24 percent. Cocoa powder offers a convenient way to get a rich chocolate flavor in baked goods, and it is the one type of chocolate that will work when you discover, halfway through a recipe, that you won't have enough melted chocolate. If the recipe calls for 1 ounce of unsweetened chocolate, simply use 3 tablespoons of cocoa powder mixed with 1 tablespoon of vegetable oil as a substitute.

unsweetened dutch-process cocoa powder

Dutch-process cocoa does not refer to a brand name but to the homeland of its creator. A Dutchman named Coenraad van Houten discovered the process of adding harmless alkali to cocoa to neutralize its natural acidity, making it less astringent. Advocates say the chocolate flavor is more well rounded; detractors call it dull. It does deepen the color, giving recipes in which it's used a rich, dark intensity. This is one reason I often substitute a small amount of Dutch-process for natural cocoa powder in a recipe.

cacao nibs

Cacao beans are used to make chocolate, and cacao nibs are produced by toasting and crushing the beans. Nibs are unsweetened, crunchy, and intensely flavored. They are not sweet but they make a wonderful addition to the home cook's repertoire of dark chocolate ingredients. I add them to baked goods whenever I need a little crunch. Caramelized, they make a marvelous snack. Cacao nibs are available in many specialty supermarket baking sections (Scharffen Berger is a popular brand) or online (see Sources, page 192).

---

got milk?

In the 1870s, while Swiss chemist Henri Nestlé was discovering how to evaporate milk into a powder, his neighbor, chocolate-maker Daniel Peter, was experimenting with new chocolate products. Their combined efforts resulted in the world's first milk chocolate candy bar and propelled this form of cacao into the world's most widely consumed chocolate.

TAKE TWO CHOCOLATES AND CALL ME IN THE MORNING

Let's refill that prescription. Whether you enjoy it by the bar or by the brownie, you've probably wondered if the claims that dark chocolate is good for your health have any basis. Here is the wonderful, deep, dark truth.

Cacao beans have a higher percentage of antioxidants than either green tea or red wine. (I'll toast to that.) The percentage is even higher than that of prunes! Consequently, the higher your chocolate's cacao content (check the percentage on the label), the better it is for you. Those antioxidants attack the destructive molecules linked to heart disease and other ailments.

Dark chocolate contains plant flavonoids, which help keep choles-terol from gathering in your blood vessels by stimulating the release _____ dilate blood vessels and increase blood flow, which, in turn, _____

responses that lead to clogged arteries. Flavonoids also help to lower the risk of lung cancer, prostate cancer, asthma, and type 2 diabetes. (Pass me another chunk of dark chocolate, *please*. I know. I know. Therapeuti-cally, we're talking about an ounce a day—no more. I can live with that.)

Chocolate provides another key to our heart: phenylethylamine or PEA. Related to amphetamines, it's shown to relieve depression and is present in higher doses in our brains when we fall in love (and during orgasm). No wonder we have a feeling of well-being.

Modern science has identified other organic compounds that explain chocolate's stimulating and mood-enhancing effects. The most common, caffeine, is a familiar daily drug for coffee and cola drinkers, although the amount of caffeine contained in chocolate is much less than that in coffee—to match the amount of caffeine you would get by drink-ing an 8-ounce cup of coffee, you'd have to eat a pound of chocolate.

But yes, you can have too much of a good thing. Like many other foods we enjoy as indulgences, chocolate has welcome healthful ben-efits, but that's not the whole picture. Chocolate is also loaded with fat and calories (an ounce of dark chocolate has between 11 and 13 grams of fat and between 150 and 170 calories), so here comes *that* word again—moderation.

I CRAVE, YOU RAVE, WE ALL LOVE DARK CHOCOLATE

Remember the familiar candy slogan "It melts in your mouth, not in your hands"? This helps to explain one of chocolate's delicious qualities and perhaps one of the main reasons we love it so much. It has to do with body heat.

Cocoa butter stays firm up to temperatures of 92°F, so in most climates, chocolate holds its shape nicely—that is, until you pop it into your mouth. Since the temperature of the human mouth is just a few degrees warmer than the melting point of cocoa butter, chocolate softens slowly, releasing its delectable flavors into—rather than merely *in*—your mouth. Dark chocolate is like a kiss from someone you really love.

CHOCOLATE TERMINOLOGY

Chocolate is enjoying a renaissance. And along with its resurgence, unfamiliar terms are emerging. Have you noticed the change in chocolate labels? Similar to labels for coffee or fine wine, they give vintages, varietals, and other details. If you find yourself floundering in a sea of percentages, origins, and tasting-note descriptions, this abbreviated list will help you understand some of the more popular terms. For in-depth information and where to buy, see Sources (page 192).

black cocoa	Available from King Arthur Flour, it is cocoa that has been highly "Dutched," or alkalized. Ever wonder what makes an Oreo cookie so dark? Now you know; see Sources (page 192).
bloom	This is a grayish-white film that forms on chocolate and indicates that temperature fluctuations occurred during storage. It should not affect the quality of the chocolate if the chocolate is to be melted and used in a recipe.
	l"ke COW" We love this tropical evergreen tree called beans) apiece. The pods grow on the trunks chocolate tree as well as on its older branches.
cacao nibs	Roasted, hulled, and broken cacao beans, nibs are the latest chocolate ingredient to enter chocolate lovers' repertoires. Intensely flavorful, nibs can be crushed, infused, caramelized, or left in their natural state.
cacao seeds or beans	Also known as cocoa beans. They are the source of all forms of chocolate and cocoa.
chocolate liquor	Also known as cocoa *mass*, chocolate liquor is the liquid or paste produced when cacao beans are roasted and ground. It is the pure, roasted, and refined cacao bean with no ingredients added. The chocolate industry uses this intermediate product as the basis for its production of cocoa powder and cocoa butter.
cocoa beans	This is another term for cacao seeds. They are the source of all forms of chocolate and cocoa.
cocoa butter	The naturally occurring, yellowish-white fat present in cacao seeds. Like all fats, it carries flavor (in this case, chocolate) to our taste buds. It is the main ingredient of white chocolate and is also used as an ingredient in cosmetics, tanning oils, and soap.

couverture

Also known as *coating chocolate*, this is dark chocolate with a high cocoa-butter content. Professional confectioners or candy makers use it for dipping and enrobing.

criollo

Native to Central America, the Caribbean islands, and South America, *criollo* is one of the three main varieties of the cultivated cacao tree. While it is the most finicky to grow, its beans are considered the finest and most aromatic, and they contribute unique secondary notes from a broad palette of flavors.

forastero

Another of the three main varieties of the cultivated cacao tree, *forastero* is the workhorse. Believed to be native to the Amazon basin, it is hardy and high-yielding, producing more than 80 percent of the world's production of cacao beans. While the beans have a big chocolate flavor, they lack the subtle nuances associated with premium chocolate.

ganache

A versatile blend of chocolate and cream (or any water-based liquid). Depending upon the temperature and the proportion of cream to chocolate, ganache can be a velvety sauce to serve over ice cream. It can also cover a cake in a shiny glaze or fluffy frosting or become as firm and toothsome as fudge.

milk chocolate

While this type of chocolate may be America's candy-bar star, it should not be used as a substitute for dark chocolate. It needs to contain only 10 percent chocolate liquor, which is why it does not have a pronounced chocolate flavor and why it plays a minor role in baking. (It also contains cocoa butter, vanilla, milk solids, and lecithin, a natural emulsifier.)

percentage

This is a useful label for gauging sweetness (or bitterness). It represents the *combined* amount, by weight, of ground cacao beans and cocoa butter in the solid chocolate, versus sugar and other ingredients. In premium chocolates, that fraction is made up solely from ground cacao beans, but some chocolate makers may add more cocoa butter than is naturally present in the beans. When that happens the flavor is not as intense, although the percentage remains the same.

single-origin, vintage, and plantation or estate chocolate	These terms are used for chocolate made from the cacao beans of a single country, region, year, or plantation. While most chocolates are a blend of beans from different regions, these chocolates are like fine wines, with distinct flavors characteristic of a particular soil and climate.
tasting terminology	In the world of premium chocolate, terms are as elaborate as the descriptive words used for wine and fine-quality coffee. Flavor and aroma profiles exist. If you're interested in learning more, see Sources (page 192).
tempering	This is the process of alternately cooling and reheating melted chocolate to form fat crystals and stabilize them within the cocoa butter, so that the solid chocolate retains its glossy sheen, snap, and melting properties.
theobroma cacao	The Latin name for the spindly tree that grows in equatorial regions of the world. Its common name is *cacao*, or simply the chocolate tree. *Theobroma* means "food of the gods," a name bestowed by botanist Carolus Linnaeus in 1753.
trinitario	One of three main varieties of the cultivated cacao tree, *trinitario* is a hybrid of *criollo* and *forastero*. It exhibits properties of both, such as high yield and aromatic beans.
white chocolate	This isn't really chocolate at all, because it contains no chocolate liquor or solids. It does contain cocoa butter with sugar, milk solids, and vanilla added. Premium-quality white chocolate, such as Green & Black's, Valrhona, Callebaut, or El Rey, has a creamy, custardlike flavor.

a word about the bean

Cocoa content—the percentages—does not guarantee a quality chocolate. It's all about the bean. An inferior bean will not make a superior chocolate no matter how high the cocoa content.

baking tips

AND DEEP, DARK CHOCOLATE

secrets

(*Read this first*, before the recipes)

Buying, storing, chopping, measuring, and melting dark chocolate: The basic how-to guide

BUYING DARK CHOCOLATE

I hope this book encourages you to begin experimenting in the kitchen with fine-quality, premium chocolates you enjoy eating instead of using semisweet and bittersweet chocolates from the supermarket's baking aisle.

Any solid, dark chocolate can be used as a baking chocolate. Remember, when a recipe highlights chocolate, the better the chocolate, the better the recipe will turn out. Begin by trying celebrated brands such as Scharffen Berger, Valrhona, Callebaut, El Rey, Michel Cluizel, Pralus, and Dagoba to find out which chocolates you enjoy eating, then branch out. You'll soon discover that no two chocolates taste alike, and a universe of new stars is waiting to be discovered.

Here's an idea: The next time you try your favorite brownie recipe, take a tiny taste of the chocolate first; it won't be missed. Then, taste the brownie. See if you can detect the same characteristics that made that premium chocolate bar so good. Was it altered? Was it improved?

STORING DARK CHOCOLATE

Properly stored, dark chocolate will keep for up to a year. Store it in a cool (60° to 70°F), dry place, and wrap it tightly in plastic wrap to protect it. The worst enemies of a fine chocolate are air, moisture, and odors (which chocolate easily absorbs). If you refrigerate it, you're inviting condensation and any number of unwanted aromas to invade.

If you notice a grayish-white film on your stored chocolate, temperature fluctuations have occurred during storage, and the cocoa butter has melted. The film is known as *bloom*. It should not affect the quality of the chocolate if it is to be melted and used in a recipe.

If you're tempted to buy more than an immediate supply of dark chocolate, remember that chocolate does not improve with age. If you must freeze it, store the unopened chocolate packages tightly in freezer bags, which will keep for several months. When you pull out a frozen package, keep it fully wrapped in the refrigerator for several hours (but not much longer, as condensation may occur), depending on its thickness. Next, leave it out, fully wrapped, at room temperature for another several hours. Then it will be ready to use and enjoy.

Cocoa powder, too, should be kept in an airtight container in a cool, dry place, away from your spices. More fragile than solid chocolate, its flavors begin to fade after six months.

CHOPPING CHOCOLATE

Chopping chocolate in small, uniform pieces is one of the best ways to ensure a quick melt and a great dessert. When a recipe calls for chopped chocolate, I aim for ¼- to ½-inch chunks (the smaller the pieces, the sooner the chocolate will melt). A recipe may call for finely chopped chocolate because you need to use a small amount of hot liquid to melt the chocolate, and you want the chocolate to melt before the liquid cools.

To chop a thick chocolate slab, use a sharp chef's knife or cleaver. Beginning at a corner, bear down on the knife with both hands to break off a small chunk. Repeat on the other end, and so forth. Then chop the small chunks into the desired size. For easy cleanup, cover the counter with a sheet of parchment paper and place a cutting board on top. The paper acts as both a landing spot for wayward chocolate flecks and a funnel to transport the runaways to their proper place. (I have a cutting board I use only for baking. No onion, garlic, or aromatic savories allowed.)

I prefer to hand-chop chocolate, though I know many bakers who like to use a food processor, especially when they need a large amount of finely chopped chocolate.

MEASURING DARK CHOCOLATE

measuring solid chocolate

In recipes using solid chocolate, the measurement should be given by weight (ounces to pounds) not by volume (teaspoons to cups). Example: 16 ounces (1 pound) premium dark chocolate. So, for accuracy, it's helpful to have a kitchen scale. If you don't, you'll need to rely on the chocolate's packaging. Example: The label on bars of Scharffen Berger dark chocolate lists the net weight as 3 oz (ounces) or 85 g (grams). For a table of equivalents, see page 196.

measuring cocoa powder

To measure cocoa powder accurately, first stir the cocoa (or tip it back and forth), then spoon the loose cocoa into the cup until it is piled high. Use the straight side of a metal spatula or knife to level off any excess. Do not use the measuring cup as a scoop, and do not tap or press the cocoa into the cup.

MELTING DARK CHOCOLATE

Straightforward as it may seem, melting chocolate can be tricky. Here are three tried-and-true tips to remember, followed by three different techniques:

Never be in a hurry. Slower is always better when chocolate is involved.

Keep chocolate dry. Otherwise, it can seize and turn lumpy, grainy, and thick (see Seize the Day, Not the Chocolate, page 25).

Chocolate scorches easily, causing it to develop a grainy texture and a burnt taste. While dark chocolate can withstand higher temperatures than milk or white chocolates, it's important to remember that you're melting the chocolate, not cooking it.

water bath

My favorite, foolproof way to melt chocolate is an oft-repeated refrain in this book. Many recipes start the same way: "Place the chocolate in a medium heatproof bowl and set in a wide pan or skillet of hot water. Set aside for 5 minutes, stirring 4 or 5 times, and let melt completely. Stir until smooth."

I learned this method of melting from reading the books of Alice Medrich, a leading authority on chocolate. While she does it on the stove top, I do it on the kitchen counter and use just-off-the-boil water from my kettle. Then I continue to gather the other ingredients needed for the recipe. Voila! By the time I'm ready to start, the chocolate is ready to use. It's never too hot, never too cold, but always perfect.

microwave

Place evenly chopped chocolate in a clean, dry microwave-able bowl. Heat, uncovered, at 50 percent power, starting with 30-second intervals, making sure to stir between intervals—remember, chocolate retains its shape and can trick you into thinking it's not melted. If necessary, after the initial time, switch to 10- to 15-second intervals to prevent scorching. When only a few lumps of chocolate are visible, remove the bowl from the microwave and stir. Enough heat will remain to complete the job.

double boiler

A double boiler is a specialized set of two fitted saucepans. The larger, bottom saucepan is partially filled with water and brought to a simmer. The smaller, upper saucepan nests inside and uses this indirect heat to melt chocolate and to cook delicate custards and sauces. You can improvise with a heatproof bowl set over a saucepan, making sure there is no gap around the rim for steam to escape and cause the chocolate to seize. Contrary to popular opinion, if the water touches the bottom of the bowl containing the chocolate, it will not ruin the chocolate (steam is hotter than boiling water). After heating the water to a simmer, I turn off the stove and let the hot water melt the chopped chocolate, stirring occasionally to hasten the process. Remember, when removing the bowl, to watch out for very hot steam.

melting chocolate with liquid

At one time or another, we all discover that if you try to melt chocolate with a small amount of liquid (or butter), it's likely to seize, or become thick and sludgy—see Seize the Day, *Not the Chocolate* (below). That's because there is not enough liquid to moisten all the dry particles within the chocolate. Since dark chocolate contains more dry particles than milk chocolate or white chocolate, it requires more water or liquid in order to melt into a smooth mixture. The rule of thumb is 1 tablespoon of liquid per ounce of chocolate.

When a recipe calls for you to melt chocolate with a liquid, make sure that the liquid is at room temperature or warmer.

seize the day, not the chocolate

Be a stickler about using dry utensils when working with chocolate. It responds noticeably to small amounts of moisture by transforming from a smooth texture to a lumpy, grainy mass. Even the smallest drop from a wet spoon has this effect. For the same reason, you should never put a lid on a pan of melting chocolate, or condensation may wreak ruin.

If the unfortunate does occur, before you toss the chocolate out, try whisking in 1 teaspoon of vegetable oil for each ounce of chocolate. Often the chocolate will smooth itself out, and the added oil won't alter your recipe. (Don't try this with butter, since it contains water.) Or, do what I sometimes do: Whisk in enough hot cream to turn a disaster into a delicious ice-cream sundae sauce.

tempering chocolate

When you buy a bar of chocolate, it has been tempered by the manufacturer so that it has a glossy sheen and an even texture. It is brittle and snaps when it's broken. Once you melt chocolate and cool it without tempering, the surface will become dull or mottled within a short time. There's no need to temper chocolate used in a batter or frosting, but if you're dipping a cookie or molding a piece of candy, you want a coating that dries hard and glossy and will last a week or more at room temperature.

The process of tempering requires practice and depends on a series of precise heating and cooling steps. The recipes in *Deep Dark Chocolate* do not require you to master this technique. Certainly, you will find dipped cookies and other dipped delights in this book, but each recipe lets you know that these sweets are best enjoyed within 3 days and should be stored at room temperature. (Since the dipping chocolate is not tempered, the coating will have a smooth, non-glossy surface. After several days, it will begin to mottle.)

Steps for success when baking or cooking with chocolate

Following a recipe can be simple and straightforward, yet it is important to follow certain steps. Easy as they may seem, they are crucial for success. The following pages describe each step and offer helpful tips so that your time in the kitchen is a pleasure and you'll have no sad surprises.

Read over the recipe before you begin.

Have all the ingredients in place, and make sure they are at room temperature.

Preheat the oven, and use an oven thermometer.

Choose the proper measuring tools, baking sheets, pots, and pans.

Have baking sheets, pots, and pans at room temperature.

Trust your eyes and instincts, jot down notes for the next time, and don't watch the clock.

READ OVER THE ENTIRE RECIPE BEFORE YOU BEGIN.

So, you've glanced at the ingredients, but did you read the instructions *all the way through*? Make it a habit before you get started. That way, you understand the sequence, the techniques, and the timing. Many recipes have recipes within them—a cake's chocolate frosting, a tart's ganache filling, a sundae's fudgy sauce. It's important that these parts come together in the right order.

If you're like me and can't wait to get started, you often overlook the amount of an ingredient called for in the first paragraph of the directions, such as the sugar used for creaming with the butter, which is only half the amount called for in the ingredients list. It turns out the other half is added along with the egg whites, way down in para-graph four—whoops! I've tipped you off by adding the word "divided" to any ingredient used in parts.

HAVE ALL THE INGREDIENTS IN PLACE, AND MAKE SURE THEY ARE AT ROOM TEMPERATURE.

Take a cue from professional bakers and cooks, who live by the French phrase *mise en place*, or "put into place." This is the excellent habit of setting out all the tools and measuring out all the ingredients before you get started.

As you read over each recipe, make sure you are using the ingredients called for and that they are at *room temperature*. Substitutions, especially when it comes to chocolate, will alter the results. Other examples? Using skim milk instead of whole milk affects tenderness, and margarine does not taste or act like butter. I've added "at room temperature" to items in the ingredients list that are likely to be chilled. Still, it is important to remember that all ingredients, unless otherwise noted, should be between 65° and 70°F.

Following is a rundown of the most elemental baking ingredients, with tips on their use and the best way to store ingredients as well as to bring them to room temperature.

butter

I use unsalted butter for baking because it has a sweeter, more delicate taste. (Salted butters, labeled "sweet cream," contain about 1/4 teaspoon of salt per stick, which can make some recipes too salty.) Store butter in the refrigerator for up to 1 month or in the freezer for up to 6 months. Since butter absorbs flavors and aromas, especially if it's unsalted, be sure it is well sealed.

At room temperature, a stick of butter gives slightly when pressed but still holds its shape. In a hurry? Cut chilled butter into small pieces and leave it out at room tempera-ture for about 15 minutes. If it's frozen, use a grater. Using the microwave is too risky: the butter melts in the middle before softening around the edges.

flour

Pillsbury and Gold Medal all-purpose unbleached flours were used in testing these recipes. Different types of flour as well as different brands have subtle differences in flavor and texture, but overall the differences are minimal. Cake flour, also known as *soft-wheat* or *Southern flour*, creates tender, fine-crumb cakes, cookies, and biscuits. When called for in this book, I used Pillsbury's Softasilk cake flour.

To measure flour accurately, first stir the flour (or tip it back and forth), then spoon the loose flour into the cup until it is piled high. Use the straight side of a metal spatula or knife to level off excess flour. Do not use the measuring cup as a scoop, and do not tap or press the flour into the cup. For best results and flavor, purchase flour in the amount you are likely to use within 6 months and store it in an airtight container at room temperature.

sugar

Granulated sugar is most commonly used in baking. Superfine sugar, also called baker's sugar, is occasionally used in a recipe or as a topping when a more delicate texture is desired. It is available in most supermarket baking sections. To make your own, you can use a processor or blender to process granulated sugar in small batches for about 30 seconds.

Powdered or confectioners' sugar is commonly used for dusting baked cookies and cakes and for making frostings. This extremely fine-grained, powdery sugar is also made from granulated sugar, mixed with small amounts of cornstarch to keep it from clumping.

Brown sugars (light or dark), which are granulated sugars enhanced with molasses, are measured by packing them firmly into the measuring cup. The recipes in this book were tested with C&H pure cane sugar (granulated, golden, brown, dark brown, powdered, and baker's).

salt

Salt brightens any recipe and helps bring out the flavors. Many types of salt are available, from the coarse kosher variety to artisan sea salts. Ordinary table salt is the best to use when baking. Its small, uniform grains flow freely and blend easily with flour and other dry ingredients.

other dry ingredients

Store dry ingredients in a cool (60° to 72°F), dry place and keep them in your pantry no longer than 6 months. Remember that, over time, spices lose their strength and flavor, and the leavening agents in baking powder become less effective. When you make a purchase, check to see if there is a "sell by" date, and keep track of these dates when you get home; add the current date to the label with a permanent marker.

eggs

Use grade AA large eggs for the recipes in this book, and use the freshest eggs possible. (Check the "sell by" date on the side of the carton.) Once you bring the eggs home, refrigerate them in their carton, not in your refrigerator's egg tray. To bring them to room temperature, take them out of the refrigerator 1 hour before using them, or place them in hot tap water for about 5 minutes.

When a recipe calls for separated eggs, separate the yolks from the whites when the eggs are cold, then let them reach room temperature. Egg whites whip best and gain the most volume when they are whisked at room temperature or slightly warmer. Be sure that your utensils are squeaky clean and without a hint of grease, which will hinder the volume of whipped eggs.

dairy

Either whole (3.5 percent fat) or low-fat (2 percent fat) milk was used to prepare the recipes calling for milk in this book. Fat-free or skim milk, with less than 1 percent fat, will alter the texture of baked goods. When a recipe calls for cream, I use heavy (whipping) cream (36 to 40 percent fat), not whipping cream (30 to 36 percent fat).

PREHEAT THE OVEN, AND USE AN OVEN THERMOMETER.

It takes 15 minutes to preheat an oven's interior to a desired and uniform temperature. Regardless of the quality of the oven, it loses its initial factory temperature calibrations over time. Since temperature is critical to the outcome of any baked good, invest in an inexpensive oven thermometer to check for accuracy. To test the recipes in this book, I used the Taylor Classic Oven Guide Thermometer (about $15).

CHOOSE THE PROPER MEASURING TOOLS, BAKING SHEETS, POTS, AND PANS.

measuring cups and spoons

There are two different types of measuring containers: dry and liquid. Dry measuring cups come in nested sets and are usually made of metal or plastic. They measure in terms of cups or portions of cups. I like to use stainless-steel cups with straight rims because they are sturdy and easy to level with a straight-edged implement.

Liquid measuring cups have spouts and graduated markers. Usually they measure in terms of cups and ounces. Liquid graduated beakers are also available. When measuring a liquid, set the cup or beaker on a level surface and let the liquid rest before reading the gauge. I own 1-cup, 2-cup, 4-cup, and 8-cup Pyrex glass measuring cups, and often use the larger ones as mixing bowls. I also use three ($\frac{1}{4}$-, 1-, and 2-cup) nifty angled measuring cups made by OXO that allow you to read measurements from above. For accuracy, use the smallest cup size that holds the amount of liquid you need.

Measuring spoons are used to measure small quantities of liquid and dry ingredients. They come in nesting sets, usually connected by a ring. The best are stainless steel with straight rims. While round spoons are most common, they also come in elongated shapes for easier entry into the narrow openings of spice jars.

Last but not least: It's a good idea to verify that your measuring cups and spoons are properly calibrated by checking their capacity against a second set of measuring tools. Make sure that the $\frac{1}{2}$-cup mark and the 1-teaspoon measure actually yield $\frac{1}{2}$ cup and 1 teaspoon.

baking sheets, cake pans, and tart pans

The best baking or cookie sheets are shiny and heavy-gauge, without raised sides or with two slightly turned-up sides. Thin sheets warp easily, and dark ones can cause cookies to over-brown. It's a good idea to have two or three baking sheets at hand so that when you're baking cookies, while one sheet is in the oven and another sheet is cooling, you can assemble the next set of cookies on the others. A jelly-roll or sheet pan resembles a cookie sheet but has four raised sides to contain batter. It's used for making pinwheel cakes, roulades, and certain bar cookies, and it's also great for corralling nuts while they're toasting in the oven.

Cake pans come in a variety of sizes, but most recipes call for either 8-inch or 9-inch round pans. Light-colored aluminum pans are preferable, since they conduct heat evenly and quickly. A springform pan is round, high, and straight-sided, with a spring-loaded hinge to release the sides of the pan from the base. This allows delicate baked goods such as cheesecakes to be easily removed. It's important to make sure the seal is tight and snug so the springform pan doesn't leak. Square and rectangular cake or baking pans are handy for brownies and other bar cookies. Choose light-colored metal or aluminum pans with 2-inch-high sides.

When it comes to tart pans, I use 9- and 11-inch shallow, tinned-steel tart pans with removable bottoms, fluted edges, and a shiny surface. By pushing up on the bottom plate with gentle pressure, you can loosen the cooked pastry away from the edges for one-piece removal. I also have a set of mini (4-inch) nonstick tart molds. Finally, when it comes to pies that go from the freezer to the oven, you'll need to use specialty ceramic pie pans such as those from Le Creuset or heavy aluminum pans (Pyrex pans won't do the trick).

The recipes in this book have been tested with the size and type of pot or pan they call for. If you need to make a substitution, be sure the pot or pan you use is a similar volume to the one specified, and be aware that you may need to adjust the baking time. You can check a pan's volume by measuring the amount of water needed to fill it.

two special tools I can't live without

HANDS: Those two handy items are always with you, and with five fingers apiece, they can tell you with your eyes shut if the dough is too sticky or as soft as a baby's bottom. They are the ultimate kitchen tool and better than any gadget. Hands are sensitive and marvelous at forming cookies, kneading dough, and letting you know with a touch when something is too hot, too cold, or just right. Use them whenever you can.

PARCHMENT PAPER: The best friend of the tidy (or messy) baker. Treated with silicone, this paper is nonstick and grease-resistant. It prevents baked goods from attaching to baking sheets and cake pans, and it makes a handy sling for removing bar cookies from the pan. A sheet of parchment paper under a mixing bowl keeps counters clean and provides a resting place for batter-coated spoons and spatulas. The paper can also act as a funnel and a landing spot for sifted ingredients. Like waxed paper, it is available in rolls in the baking section of most supermarkets. It also comes in bulk, precut sheets at retail baking-supply stores. One box containing a thousand $16\,{}^3\!/\!_8$-inch-by-24-inch sheets costs about $38 and lasts for years.

HAVE BAKING SHEETS, POTS, AND PANS AT ROOM TEMPERATURE.

After that first batch of cookies, your baking sheet will no longer be at room temperature. If you place dough on it, the hot sheet will melt the dough, causing the cookies to run and to bake improperly. To avoid this, have extra baking sheets on hand, or run room-temperature water over the underside of the baking sheet to cool it between batches. **It's best to bake cookies one sheet at a time, in the center of the oven so the oven's hot air can circulate freely around it.** This doesn't happen when the baking sheets are stacked on shelves, one above the other, or when you use a jelly-roll pan instead of a baking sheet. If you're rushed and need to bake two sheets at once, rotate them from front to back and top to bottom halfway through the baking sequence.

TRUST YOUR EYES AND INSTINCTS, JOT DOWN NOTES FOR THE NEXT TIME, AND DON'T WATCH THE CLOCK.

In this book's recipes, certain steps give visual cues as well as approximate times, such as "Bake until the muffins have risen, are lightly browned, and a tester inserted in the center comes out with a few moist crumbs, about 25 minutes."

It is important to understand that mixing and baking times are always approximate because they depend on many factors, from an individual cook's skills to an oven's accuracy. Use suggested times as guidelines, and place your faith mainly in the other signs of doneness and what you see and smell. While this is true for baking of any kind, it's especially true when you're using chocolate because the dough or batter is dark and it's often difficult to "see" when it's done. Use indicators, such as a crisp crust or a top that has "lost its sheen." Try to develop your own vocabulary of visual cues, and when you find a discrepancy, be sure to jot it down in the recipe's margin for the next time. My cookbooks are my collective kitchen diary, with notes, comments, and even dates written in the margins.

CHOCOLATE COOKIES
and
DEEP, DARK BROWNIES

chocolate
COOKIES WITH ALL
THE CHIPS

makes about
3
DOZEN
COOKIES

THIS MULTI-CHOCOLATE-CHIP TREAT IS SO CHOCK-FULL
of chips that the chocolaty dough becomes simply a vehicle (and a mighty
good one, too). I think you'll find that the combination of chips really makes this
cookie stand out; but if you don't have a variety of chips on hand, you can use
just one kind or a variety of sizes from mini to giant. Be sure to try the variation.
The addition of toasted almonds and red-wine raisins is sublime.

<table>
<tr><td>¾ cup premium semisweet chocolate chips</td><td>¼ teaspoon salt</td></tr>
<tr><td>¾ cup premium white chocolate chips</td><td>½ cup (1 stick) unsalted butter, at room temperature</td></tr>
<tr><td>¾ cup premium milk chocolate chips</td><td>½ cup firmly packed light brown sugar</td></tr>
<tr><td>1 cup all-purpose flour</td><td>¼ cup granulated sugar</td></tr>
<tr><td>½ cup premium unsweetened cocoa powder</td><td>1 large egg, at room temperature</td></tr>
<tr><td>½ teaspoon baking soda</td><td>1 teaspoon pure vanilla extract</td></tr>
</table>

Preheat the oven to 350°F. Line a baking sheet with parchment paper
or leave it ungreased.

In a small bowl, mix the semisweet, white, and milk chocolate
chips until blended. In another small bowl, whisk the flour, cocoa,
baking soda, and salt until well blended. Set aside.

In a stand mixer or with a hand mixer set on medium speed, beat
the butter until creamy. Add the brown and granulated sugars and
beat on medium speed until light and fluffy. Beat in the egg until well

continued

blended, scraping down the sides and bottom of the bowl as necessary. Beat in the vanilla until blended. On low speed, slowly add the dry ingredients and beat until just blended, again scraping down the bowl as necessary. Beat or fold in the chocolate chips until evenly distributed.

Drop the dough, by tablespoonfuls, onto the prepared baking sheet, about 2 inches apart. Bake until set and the tops have lost their sheen, about 12 minutes. (Since the dough is dark, the first batch will be the key to when the cookies are done.) Let the cookies firm and cool slightly on the baking sheet before transferring to a wire rack to cool completely. Repeat with the remaining cookie dough, reusing the parchment paper.

VARIATION

For an out-of-this-world, grown-up chocolate chipper, try **Chocolate Chip Cookies That Have It All**. Follow the main recipe, adding ⅓ cup chopped slivered toasted almonds and ⅓ cup Red-Wine Raisins (page 57) to the dough after the chocolate chips are blended. Beat until evenly blended and proceed as directed.

bittersweet chocolate–caramel
CRACKER COOKIES:
AN ASSORTMENT

makes
35
SQUARE
COOKIES

WITH THEIR FLAKY CRUST, SMOOTH CARAMEL FILLING,
and bittersweet chocolate glaze, these scrumptious bar-style cookies are rich and habit-forming. They're also just the ticket for sampling dark chocolate with a variety of new flavor partners. The additional step of garnishing the glaze with a series of toppings, sprinkled in parallel lines before the cookies are cut, makes it easy to create an array of assorted flavors.

The secret to the flaky crust? It's not complicated pie dough or layers of transparent phyllo. No, this crust is made from supermarket saltine crackers. The crackers take on a taste and appearance that would impress the most discerning cookie or chocolate connoisseur. The secret is revealed only when the baker inverts the cookies to cut them.

This recipe requires a 10-by-15-inch jelly-roll pan and a candy thermometer.

1 ¼ cups (2 ½ sticks) unsalted butter, melted, divided

35 saltine crackers, plus 7 to mark off the rows

1 cup firmly packed dark brown sugar

1 can (14 ounces) sweetened condensed milk

10 ounces premium dark chocolate, melted (see page 23)

About 1 teaspoon of one of the following toppings for each cracker row:

Fleur de sel or other sea salt

Colored or turbinado sugar

Finely ground espresso

Assorted pepper blends

Assorted spice blends or rubs

Preheat the oven to 425°F. To make removing the finished cookies easy, line a 10-by-15-inch jelly-roll pan with a sheet of aluminum foil, shiny side up, leaving a few inches hanging over the long edges.

continued

Drizzle ¼ cup of the melted butter onto the foil-lined pan and brush to cover the bottom. Arrange 35 crackers, side by side (5 by 7) and evenly spaced, so they completely cover the bottom of the pan (don't worry if there are small gaps).

In a saucepan over medium heat, combine the remaining 1 cup melted butter and the brown sugar and bring to a boil. Boil until the mixture forms a thick syrup (248°F on a candy thermometer), about 2 minutes. Remove from the heat and stir in the condensed milk until blended. Pour the mixture over the crackers, making sure all the crackers are covered.

Bake until the syrup layer bubbles, 10 to 12 minutes. Remove from the oven and drizzle the melted chocolate over the top. Using an offset metal spatula, quickly spread the glaze with a few strokes. To fill in any gaps, using oven mitts, tilt the pan back and forth. Let the glaze set for 5 minutes.

To create a guide for garnishing the crackers with a single line of topping, prop the 7 extra saltines along the lengthwise inside edge of the pan. (Don't worry, they'll come out easily after you're finished garnishing.) Using the saltines as guidelines, sprinkle a line of topping down the midsection of each cracker row. If necessary, using your fingers or the back of a spoon, lightly press the topping into the chocolate. Remove the saltine-cracker guides and freeze the pan until the chocolate sets, about 30 minutes.

Remove from the freezer and invert the pan onto a clean surface. Carefully peel back the foil to reveal the cracker underside of the cookies. Using a sharp knife, cut the cookies along the cracker outlines. This is easier to do when the cookies have begun to thaw slightly. If desired, invert the squares and cut each diagonally into 2 triangles for bite-size pieces.

VARIATION

For **Crunchy Nut Bittersweet Caramel Bars**, follow the main recipe, substituting 1 cup of your favorite toasted, chopped, or sliced nuts for the topping selections. Sprinkle the nuts over the entire surface and proceed as directed.

piedras
BLANCAS
makes about
2 1/2
DOZEN
COOKIES

NAMED AFTER AN ARGENTINEAN GLACIER HIGH IN THE

Andes, these snow-capped South American cookies resemble classic choc-olate crinkles. (Each cookie develops a crinkled white surface during the baking process.) But don't let appearances fool you. Piedras Blancas are pep-pered with chili powder, a touch of mace, and delectable bits of cacao bean (also called nibs), for an exotic heat and earthy crunch. These are definitely adult cookies.

3 ounces premium dark chocolate, chopped

1/4 cup unsalted butter, cut into pieces

1 cup all-purpose flour

3 tablespoons premium unsweetened cocoa powder

1 teaspoon baking powder

2 1/2 teaspoons chili powder or your favorite pepper blend, divided

1/2 teaspoon ground mace

1/4 teaspoon salt

2 large eggs, at room temperature

1 cup granulated sugar

1 teaspoon pure vanilla extract, preferably Mexican

3 tablespoons premium cacao nibs, chopped into small bits

1/2 cup sifted powdered sugar

Place the chocolate and butter in a medium heatproof bowl and set in a wide pan or skillet of hot water. Set aside for 5 minutes, stirring 4 or 5 times, and let the chocolate melt completely. Stir occasionally until the mixture is smooth and cools slightly. In another medium bowl, whisk the flour, cocoa, baking powder, 1 1/2 teaspoons of the chili powder, the mace, and salt until well blended. Set aside.

continued

In a stand mixer or with a hand mixer set on medium speed, beat the eggs, sugar, and vanilla until pale, 2 to 3 minutes. Alternately blend the dry ingredients and the chocolate mixture into the egg mixture in increments. Stir in the nibs. Cover and refrigerate until firm, about 3 hours.

Preheat the oven to 350°F. Line a baking sheet with parchment paper or lightly grease it.

Sift, or sprinkle using a sieve, the powdered sugar into a shallow bowl and blend in the remaining 1 teaspoon chili powder. Shape the chilled dough into 1½-inch balls and roll in the powdered-sugar mixture to form a thick coat. Place the cookies about 2 inches apart on the prepared baking sheet. Bake until set, 12 to 14 minutes. Transfer to a wire rack and let cool completely.

triple chocolate—
SPANISH PEANUT
COOKIES

makes about
2 1/2
DOZEN COOKIES

LISA ALLEN, BAKER AND CO-OWNER OF THE PACIFIC WAY
Bakery and Café in Gearhart, Oregon, created these rich, semisoft chocolate cookies years ago when she had a surplus of Spanish peanuts left over from an ice cream–making experiment. Lisa discovered just how well a salty ingredient complements chocolate. Now, it's your turn. Just so you know, the recipe can easily be doubled.

These dipped cookies are best enjoyed within 3 days and should be stored at room temperature. (Since the dipping chocolate is not tempered, the coating will have a smooth, non-glossy surface. After several days, it will begin to mottle.) Undipped cookies can be stored in an airtight container for up to 2 weeks or frozen for up to 2 months.

1 cup premium semisweet chocolate chips

1 cup salted and roasted Spanish peanuts

1 cup all-purpose flour

1/2 cup premium unsweetened cocoa powder

1/2 teaspoon baking soda

1/4 teaspoon salt

1/2 cup plus 2 tablespoons unsalted butter, at room temperature

1/2 cup granulated sugar

1/2 cup firmly packed light brown sugar

1 large egg, at room temperature

1/2 teaspoon pure vanilla extract

6 ounces premium dark chocolate, melted (see page 23)

Preheat the oven to 350°F. Line a baking sheet with parchment paper or leave it ungreased.

continued

In a medium bowl, mix the chocolate chips and Spanish peanuts until blended. In another medium bowl, whisk the flour, cocoa, baking soda, and salt until well blended. Set aside.

In a stand mixer or with a hand mixer set on low speed, beat the butter until creamy. Add the granulated and brown sugars and beat on medium speed until light and fluffy. Beat in the egg until well blended, scraping down the sides and bottom of the bowl as necessary. Beat in the vanilla until blended. On low speed, slowly add the dry ingredients and beat until just blended, again scraping down the bowl as necessary. Stir in the chocolate-peanut mixture.

Drop the dough, by rounded tablespoonfuls, onto the prepared baking sheet about 2 inches apart. Bake until set and the tops have lost their sheen, about 12 minutes. Pull the parchment paper with the cookies onto the counter and let the cookies firm and cool slightly before transferring from the parchment to a wire rack to cool completely. (If not using parchment, let the cookies firm and cool slightly on the baking sheet before transferring.) Repeat with the remaining cookie dough, reusing the parchment paper.

Meanwhile, place 2 wire racks on a sheet of parchment or waxed paper to catch any chocolate drips. Dip half of each cookie into the melted chocolate. Place the cookies on the racks to set, for up to 2 hours, depending on room temperature. For a fast set, after 10 minutes, you can slip the wire rack into the refrigerator to chill for no longer than 5 minutes.

VARIATION

My kids love my **Lunchbox Chocolate–Spanish Peanut Cookies**. Follow the main recipe, stirring in ½ cup raisins with the chocolate chips and Spanish peanuts until blended. Proceed as directed, but eliminate dipping the finished cookie in chocolate.

black magic
CHOCOLATE ESPRESSO
COOKIES

makes about
4
DOZEN COOKIES

JAVA GURU JIM ROBERTS, COFOUNDER OF COFFEE PEOPLE, created these supernatural cookies to carry in his northwest coffeehouses. Ultra-chocolaty, they're big, bold, and rich, with jolts of bittersweet chocolate and espresso. High-energy, adult cookies, they are slightly crunchy on the outside with a scrumptious soft center loaded with chips.

If you don't have access to an espresso machine, it's fine to use 2 teaspoons of instant espresso, such as Medaglia d'Oro, to 1 ounce of hot water.

16 ounces (1 pound) premium dark chocolate, chopped

2 ounces premium unsweetened baking chocolate, chopped

¾ cup (1½ sticks) unsalted butter, cut into pieces

2 cups all-purpose flour

2 teaspoons baking soda

½ teaspoon salt

1½ cups firmly packed light brown sugar

1 cup granulated sugar, divided, plus more if needed

3 to 4 tablespoons espresso (see headnote)

2 teaspoons pure vanilla extract

4 large eggs, at room temperature

1 cup premium semisweet chocolate chips

1 cup premium milk chocolate chips

⅓ cup very finely ground espresso coffee beans (see Note, page 46)

Powdered sugar for dusting (optional)

Preheat the oven to 325°F. Line a baking sheet with parchment paper or lightly grease it.

Place the dark and unsweetened chocolates and the butter in a medium heatproof bowl and set in a wide pan or skillet of hot water. Set aside for 5 minutes, stirring 4 or 5 times, and let melt completely.

continued

Stir until smooth. In another medium bowl, whisk the flour, baking soda, and salt until well blended. Set aside.

Transfer the chocolate mixture to a stand mixer and add the brown sugar and ⅔ cup of the granulated sugar. Beat on medium speed until well blended. The mixture will appear grainy. Add the espresso and vanilla and beat until blended. Beat in the eggs, one at a time, until fully blended, scraping down the sides and bottom of the bowl as necessary. On low speed, slowly add the dry ingredients and beat until just blended, again scraping down the bowl as necessary. Do not overbeat. Beat or fold in the semisweet and milk chocolate chips until blended. Let the dough rest for about 20 minutes, until it thickens and is easy to scoop, or refrigerate until slightly chilled, checking frequently. Meanwhile, in a small bowl, combine the remaining ⅓ cup granulated sugar and the ground espresso.

Scoop up about 2 tablespoons of the dough and gingerly roll it between your hands to form a 1½-inch ball (if the dough sticks to your hands, keep a bowl of cold water nearby and occasionally dip your hands, shaking off the excess). Drop the ball into the sugar-espresso mixture and roll to coat. Place on the prepared baking sheet and flatten slightly. Repeat to make more cookies, placing them 2½ to 3 inches apart on the pan.

Bake until slightly firm and the tops are cracked and dull, 12 to 15 minutes. (The first batch may take about 15 minutes, but as the dough thickens, the cooking time decreases.) Pull the parchment paper with the cookies onto the counter and let the cookies firm and cool slightly before transferring to a wire rack to cool completely. (If not using parchment, let the cookies firm and cool slightly on the baking sheet before transferring.) When cool, dust with powdered sugar, if desired. Repeat with the remaining cookie dough, reusing the parchment paper.

NOTE

What you need here is superfine coffee powder, typically called Turkish grind on commercial machines. For authentic Turkish coffee, you can use a hand-held Turkish grinder, or ask your coffee shop or vendor to grind it for you.

baby LOVES

makes
24
SANDWICH
COOKIES

I CALL THEM "BABY LOVES," BECAUSE THE FIRST TIME I MADE
these delicate pink-macaroon-and-ganache cookies was for the celebration of a
chocolate-loving mother-to-be and her friends. The recipe comes from Dominique
Guelin, Oregon's favorite French baker and the owner of Portland's St. Honoré
Boulangerie. The ganache is my choice. As I was shopping for ingredients I spied
a bar of Dagoba chocolate called Roseberry. Once I took a bite and savored the
gentle perfume of rosemary and rose hips, I knew it would create the perfect
filling. Dagoba is available where most fine chocolate bars are sold.

MACAROONS
³/₄ cup slivered almonds (about
   3¼ ounces)

1 cup plus 2 tablespoons powdered sugar

2 large egg whites, at room
   temperature or slightly warm

3 tablespoons plus 1 teaspoon
   granulated sugar

1 or 2 drops red or pink food coloring

FILLING
1 bar (2 ounces) Dagoba Roseberry
   (59%, with raspberries) or other
   premium dark chocolate, chopped

¼ cup heavy (whipping) cream

TO MAKE THE MACAROONS: Line 2 baking sheets with parchment paper.
On each sheet, using a dark pencil, draw twenty-four 1½-inch circles,
4 across and 6 down. Turn the parchment over, pencil side down (you
should be able to see the circles you drew through the paper). Set aside.

In a food processor, process the almonds in short bursts until
finely ground. Add the powdered sugar and continue to process in
short bursts until the almond meal is as fine as possible. Transfer the
almond mixture to a medium bowl.

continued

In a stand mixer fitted with the whisk attachment, whisk the egg whites on medium-low speed until foamy. Increase the speed to medium-high and gradually add the granulated sugar. Beat until soft peaks form. Fold the almond mixture and food coloring into the egg whites until no large streaks of egg white remain and the color is uniform.

Transfer the mixture to a pastry bag fitted with a ¼-inch tip. (While you can use a 1-quart zippered plastic bag with one bottom corner cut slightly less than ¼ inch, it doesn't give the same control.) With one hand perpendicular to a prepared baking sheet, rest the tip in the center of a pencil circle and apply even pressure to the end of the bag. Slowly pull the bag up from the baking sheet to pipe a 1½-inch round macaroon, lifting up the bag in a circular motion to release the top of the macaroon. Repeat to fill all the circles on both baking sheets. Let rest for 30 minutes to form a skin.

Preheat the oven to 300°F. Bake the macaroons, one sheet at a time, until crisp on the outside and moist on the inside, 8 to 10 minutes (do not open the oven during baking).

Pull the parchment onto the counter or wire racks and let the macaroons cool for 10 minutes. Removing the cookies can be a bit tricky. If they don't come off easily (and they usually don't), turn the paper over on a dry surface. The macaroons will not fall off. Moisten the parchment under each macaroon with a damp paper towel. Turn over and let sit for 2 to 3 minutes. Then, carefully peel the macaroons off the parchment by sliding a thin knife underneath. The macaroons can be stored in an airtight container for several days.

TO MAKE THE FILLING: Place the chocolate and cream in a medium heatproof bowl and set in a wide pan or skillet of hot water. Set aside for 5 minutes, stirring 4 or 5 times, and let the chocolate melt completely. Stir until smooth. Let stand to thicken to a spreading consistency or refrigerate until slightly chilled, checking frequently.

TO ASSEMBLE: Spread the base of 1 macaroon with the filling and sandwich together with another macaroon. Repeat with the remaining macaroons. The cookies can be refrigerated in an airtight container up to 2 days.

he-loves-me-not VALENTINE HEARTS

makes about 2 DOZEN 2-INCH COOKIES

IT'S A GOOD THING. REALLY. A friend was visiting from San Francisco. It was Valentine's Day weekend, and she had just found out her sweetheart was sweet on someone else. So we decided to bake our way through the romantic holiday and eat every last crumb. What better way to begin than with a dark chocolate shortbread cookie heart made with his favorite nuts? We dipped each cookie in really good deep, dark chocolate before devouring the hearts, but they are also delicious plain and simple.

Does your heart drop every time you try to roll out cookie dough? Mine did until I discovered the old-fashioned pastry cloth and rolling-pin cover. To my mind, these are among the most valuable tools in a baker's kitchen. Now, rolled-out cookies or pie crusts are a breeze, and they never stick.

Almond meal, or finely ground almonds, is available at Trader Joe's and natural-foods stores or supermarket aisles. These dipped cookies are best enjoyed within 3 days and should be stored at room temperature. (Since the dipping chocolate is not tempered, the coating will have a smooth, non-glossy surface. After several days, it will begin to mottle.)

COOKIES
1 cup all-purpose flour
¼ cup almond meal
¼ cup premium unsweetened cocoa powder
1 tablespoon premium unsweetened Dutch-process cocoa powder
Large pinch of salt
½ cup (1 stick) unsalted butter, at room temperature

½ cup granulated sugar
Scant ¼ teaspoon pure almond or vanilla extract

DIPPING CHOCOLATE
3 ounces premium dark chocolate, chopped
1 teaspoon vegetable shortening

continued

TO MAKE THE COOKIES: In a medium bowl, whisk the flour, almond meal, unsweetened and Dutch-process cocoas, and salt until well blended. Set aside.

In a stand mixer or with a hand mixer set on medium speed, beat the butter until creamy. Add the sugar and beat on medium speed until light and fluffy. Beat in the almond extract until well blended, scraping down the sides and bottom of the bowl as necessary. On low speed, slowly add the dry ingredients and beat until just blended, again scraping down the bowl as necessary. Lay a sheet of plastic wrap on the counter and scrape the crumbly dough onto one-half of the wrap. Fold the wrap over the dough and knead 3 or 4 times. Flatten the dough into a disk in the plastic wrap and refrigerate for 20 minutes.

Preheat the oven to 300°F. Line a baking sheet with parchment paper or leave it ungreased.

Remove the dough disk from the refrigerator, unwrap it, and cut it in half.

On a pastry cloth or a lightly floured board with a cloth-covered rolling pin or between 2 sheets of heavy-duty plastic wrap, roll out one-half of the dough to a ¼-inch thickness. Using a 2-inch heart-shaped cookie cutter, cut a cookie, pressing the cutter straight down into the dough. Repeat, cutting the cookies closely together to avoid rerolling. Using a spatula, carefully transfer the cookies to the prepared baking sheet about 1 inch apart. Bake for 12 minutes, then rotate the cookie sheet and bake until firm to the touch, about 12 minutes longer. Repeat with the remaining dough.

Pull the parchment paper with the cookies onto the counter and let the cookies firm and cool slightly before transferring from the parchment to a wire rack to cool completely. (If not using parchment, let the cookies firm and cool slightly on the baking sheet before transferring.) Undipped cookies can be stored in an airtight container for up to 2 weeks or frozen for up to 2 months.

TO MAKE THE DIPPING CHOCOLATE: Place the chocolate and shortening in a small, deep heatproof bowl and set in a wide pan or skillet of hot water. Set aside for 5 minutes, stirring 4 or 5 times, and let the chocolate melt completely. Stir until smooth.

Meanwhile, place 2 wire racks on a sheet of parchment or waxed paper to catch any chocolate drips. Dip half of each cookie into the chocolate and allow the extra chocolate to drip back into the bowl. Place the cookies on the racks to set, for up to 2 hours, depending on room temperature. For a fast set, after 10 minutes, you can slip the wire rack into the refrigerator to chill for no longer than 5 minutes.

VARIATION

Don't wait until Hanukkah to make **Nibby Hanukkah Coins**. Follow the main recipe. After rolling out the dough, use a 1½-inch plain round cutter to form each cookie. After transferring to the prepared baking sheet, lightly press 3 to 5 cacao nibs into the center of each "coin." Bake as directed, cutting the time to 20 minutes. When the cookies are cooled, dip half of each cookie into the chocolate but do not cover the nibs. Proceed as directed.

good ol' FUDGY BROWNIES

makes 16 SMALL BROWNIES

A FUDGY BROWNIE IS NOT FUDGE. IT DOESN'T NEED frosting, and it is never dolled up with chips and chunks. A fudgy brownie is an effortless ode to deep, dark chocolate, a two-bowl affair where the simple stir of a wooden spoon conjures up sweet dreams of warm brownie à la mode. This is a comfort brownie with an intense chocolate punch.

5 ounces premium dark chocolate, chopped

½ cup (1 stick) unsalted butter, cut into pieces

¼ cup premium unsweetened cocoa powder

1 cup granulated sugar

Pinch of salt

2 large eggs, at room temperature

½ cup all-purpose flour

Preheat the oven to 350°F. Lightly grease an 8-by-8-inch baking pan with cooking spray. To make removing the finished brownies easy, line the pan lengthwise and widthwise with two 7½-by-16-inch sheets of parchment paper or aluminum foil, shiny side up, and use the overhang as handles.

Place the chocolate and butter in a medium heatproof bowl and set in a wide pan or skillet of hot water. Set aside for 5 minutes, stirring 4 or 5 times, and let the chocolate melt completely. Stir until smooth. Remove from the heat and whisk in the cocoa powder, sugar, and salt. Whisk in the eggs, and then stir in the flour until just blended. Scrape the batter into the prepared baking pan and spread evenly. Bake until a tester inserted in the center comes out with a few moist crumbs

continued

clinging to it, about 35 minutes. Do not overbake. Transfer to a wire rack and let the brownies cool completely, then lift from the pan using the overhanging parchment. Cut into squares.

VARIATION

If you want to glam up your brownies, try **Good Ol' Fudgy Brownies with Chocolate-Scented Powdered Sugar** (shown in the photo on page 54).

TO MAKE THE SCENTED SUGAR: In a bowl, whisk 2 cups powdered sugar and ½ cup premium cacao nibs until blended. Place in an airtight container for several weeks. When ready to use, sift the sugar through a fine sieve to capture the nibs.

TO MAKE THE BROWNIES: Follow the main recipe. After the brownies cool completely (or after they're cut into squares), dust the top with chocolate-scented powdered sugar. Feel free to use the cacao nibs to bake with after the sugar is gone.

scharffen berger
BROWNIES WITH RED-WINE RAISINS
AND TOASTED WALNUTS

makes
9
MEDIUM
BROWNIES

THESE BROWNIES ARE A HAPPY MEDIUM BETWEEN FUDGY (read "decadent") and cakey (read "genteel"), and they're versatile. If you want to add extra tastes by including raisins, nuts, or chocolate chips, they are the ideal brownies to experiment with. I like to use Scharffen Berger for the chocolate and the cocoa and dress the brownies up with plump, drunk raisins and lightly toasted walnuts or hazelnuts. See what you think, then have fun coming up with your own additions. Remember: For brownies to be at their best, don't overbeat the batter.

RAISINS
½ cup raisins
½ cup good, dry red wine

BROWNIES
5 ounces Scharffen Berger bittersweet chocolate or other premium dark chocolate, chopped
½ cup plus 2 tablespoons all-purpose flour
¼ cup Scharffen Berger unsweetened cocoa powder or other premium unsweetened cocoa powder

¼ teaspoon baking powder
¼ teaspoon salt
½ cup plus 2 tablespoons unsalted butter, at room temperature
1 cup granulated sugar
3 large eggs, at room temperature
½ teaspoon pure vanilla extract
½ cup lightly toasted walnuts, coarsely chopped

TO MAKE THE RAISINS: At least 12 hours before making the brownies, combine the raisins and red wine in a jar with a lid. Cover, gently shake, and let the raisins soak overnight. To use, drain the raisins, but

continued

do not get rid of the wine. Taste it! You'll find a good use for it, such as a dessert sauce for poached fruit or a portlike cordial.

TO MAKE THE BROWNIES: Preheat the oven to 350°F. Lightly grease an 8-by-8-inch baking pan with cooking spray. To make removing the brownies easy, line the pan lengthwise and widthwise with two 7-by-12-inch sheets of parchment paper or aluminum foil, shiny side up, and use the overhang as handles.

Place the chocolate in a small heatproof bowl and set in a wide pan or skillet of hot water. Set aside for 5 minutes, stirring 4 or 5 times, and let it melt completely. Stir until smooth. In a medium bowl, whisk the flour, cocoa, baking powder, and salt until well blended. Set aside.

With a stand or hand mixer set on low speed, beat the butter and sugar in a medium bowl until well blended. Beat in the eggs, one at a time, until fully blended, scraping down the sides and bottom of the bowl as necessary. Beat in the vanilla until blended. Alternately blend the dry ingredients and the melted chocolate into the egg mixture in increments. Using a rubber spatula or wooden spoon, fold in the raisins and walnuts. Stop when the ingredients are just blended. Scrape the batter into the prepared baking pan and spread evenly. Bake about 35 minutes, until a tester inserted in the center comes out clean or with a few moist crumbs clinging to it. Transfer to a wire rack and let the brownies cool completely, then lift from the pan using the overhanging parchment. Cut into squares.

I'LL HAVE MY CAKE
and
EAT YOURS, TOO

"IT'S MY PARTY" BIRTHDAY CAKE
62

AUNT TRUDY'S IRRESISTIBLE
CHOCOLATE ZUCCHINI CAKE
66

state fair chocolate layer cake
69

ONE-BITE-TO-HEAVEN CHOCOLATE YEAST CAKE
72

PAPA HAYDN'S CHOCOLATE GÂTEAU
75

CHOCOLATE GINGERBREAD
WITH CACAO-NIB WHIPPED CREAM
77

Lamington Cakes
80

WEDDING CUPCAKES WITH
WEDDING-PARTY FROSTINGS
84

six tall chocolate–sour cream cupcakes
90

"it's my party" BIRTHDAY CAKE

Serves 10 TO 12

MAKES ONE 8-INCH
LAYER CAKE

BEHIND EVERY HAPPY BIRTHDAY IS A CELEBRATION CAKE— the kind that looks grand and tastes great. Here is mine: four layers of moist, tender chocolate cake filled and topped with dark chocolate frosting; a crowning layer of white chocolate and cacao-nib ganache that's tinted pink; and loads of candles (well, forty max). When it comes to candle holders, have fun. Try delicate, candied rose petals or individual chocolate truffles (page 166).

Adding the Dutch-process cocoa powder to the cake batter and the frosting gives both a darker color. None around? It's fine to leave it out.

GANACHE
1 cup heavy (whipping) cream
2 tablespoons premium cacao nibs, chopped into bits
Small pinch of salt
6 ounces premium white chocolate such as Green & Black's, Valrhona, Callebaut, or El Rey, finely chopped
1 drop of red food coloring, or more if desired

CAKE
2 cups cake flour
²⁄₃ cup premium unsweetened cocoa powder
2 tablespoons premium unsweetened Dutch-process cocoa powder (optional)
1¼ teaspoons baking soda
½ teaspoon salt

¾ cup (1½ sticks) unsalted butter, at room temperature, plus more for the pans
1²⁄₃ cups granulated sugar
3 large eggs, at room temperature
1 teaspoon pure vanilla extract
1⅓ cups water

FROSTING
1 pound cream cheese, at room temperature, cut into pieces
1 cup (2 sticks) unsalted butter, at room temperature, cut into pieces
1 cup sifted powdered sugar
½ cup premium unsweetened cocoa powder
2 tablespoons premium unsweetened Dutch-process cocoa powder (optional)
1 teaspoon pure vanilla extract
Pinch of salt

TO MAKE THE GANACHE: At least 8 hours or up to 3 days before assembling the cake, in a small saucepan over medium-high heat, combine the cream, nibs, and salt and bring the mixture to a simmer. Remove from the heat, cover, and steep for 30 minutes. Strain the cream through a fine-mesh sieve and discard the nibs. Place the white chocolate in a small heatproof bowl. Reheat the cream over medium-high heat until tiny bubbles form around the edges, then pour it over the chocolate. Let stand for several minutes, then stir until the chocolate is melted and the mixture is smooth. Stir in the red food coloring (if you need more, use a toothpick's tip to dip a speck more coloring into the ganache until it reaches the desired color). Cover and refrigerate the mixture for at least 8 hours or up to 3 days. Set aside the red food coloring until you're ready to assemble the cake.

TO MAKE THE CAKE: Preheat the oven to 350°F. Lightly butter the bottom and sides of two 8-inch round cake pans. Line the bottom of each pan with a round of parchment or waxed paper. In a medium bowl, whisk the flour, the unsweetened cocoa and the Dutch-process cocoa (if using), the baking soda, and salt until well blended.

In a stand or hand mixer set on medium speed, beat the butter until creamy. Add the sugar and beat until light, fluffy, and nearly white, about 5 minutes. Beat in the eggs, one at a time, until fully blended, scraping down the sides and bottom of the bowl as necessary. Beat in the vanilla until blended. Add the dry ingredients, alternating with the water, in several increments, and beat until just blended and smooth. Scrape down the bowl again.

Divide the batter between the prepared pans and spread evenly. Gently rotate the pans to settle and level the batter. Bake until the cakes are springy to the touch and a tester inserted in the center comes out with a few moist crumbs clinging to it, 35 to 40 minutes. Let the layers cool in their pans on a wire rack for at least 15 minutes. Gently loosen the edges with a thin knife before inverting the layers onto the racks. Let the cakes cool thoroughly, about 2 hours, before carefully peeling off the parchment to frost them.

continued

TO MAKE THE FROSTING: Make sure the cream cheese and butter are not too warm or the frosting will be too soft. In a medium bowl, gently whisk the powdered sugar, the unsweetened cocoa, and the Dutch-process cocoa (if using), until well blended.

With a stand or hand mixer set on low speed, beat the cream cheese, butter, vanilla, and salt until well blended. Slowly add the powdered-sugar mixture and beat until smooth. Finish by increasing the speed to medium-high for 30 seconds.

TO ASSEMBLE THE CAKE: Place a dollop of frosting in the middle of a cake stand. To create 4 layers, using a long, serrated knife, carefully slice the 2 cake layers horizontally in half. (To make moving the tender layers easier, slide each onto a disposable plastic plate with the upturned edges of the plate cut off.) Place 1 layer on the stand, top side up, and, using an offset spatula, spread ⅔ cup frosting evenly over the top. Top with another layer, cut side up, and spread with another 1 cup frosting. Repeat with the third cake layer. Place the top (fourth) layer on top, bottom side up, and brush off any large, loose crumbs. Spread a thin layer of frosting over the top and sides of the cake to seal in the remaining crumbs. Refrigerate the cake for 1 hour, leaving the remaining frosting at room temperature. Spread the remaining frosting evenly over the top and sides of the cake. Let set for several hours before applying the ganache. The cake can be frosted 1 day ahead and stored in a cake keeper at cool (60° to 70°F) room temperature.

When you are ready to apply the ganache, whip it until it holds a nice shape. Do not overbeat. Using an offset spatula, spread a thick layer of the ganache over the chocolate frosting. (If the ganache becomes stiff, warm the spatula under warm water and dry completely.) The cake is ready to decorate as desired.

aunt trudy's irresistible
CHOCOLATE ZUCCHINI
CAKE

serves

8

MAKES ONE 9-INCH
ROUND CAKE

WE ALL HAVE AN AUNT TRUDY IN OUR LIVES—THE PERSON
who can't help but share a garden's worth of homegrown zucchini. But zucchini bread is a little like fruitcake: You can pass around only so much. Here's my idea: Use the surplus zucchini to make a moist and delectable dark chocolate cake that even your kids will welcome.

For a quick snack, dust the top of the warm cake with powdered sugar. To elevate it to the status of dinnertime dessert, frost it with a slightly tangy chocolate-cream cheese frosting.

CAKE

1½ cups grated zucchini (about 2 medium)

¾ cup peeled and grated carrot (about 2 medium)

1¼ cups all-purpose flour

⅓ cup premium unsweetened cocoa powder

1 tablespoon premium unsweetened Dutch-process cocoa powder

¾ teaspoon baking soda

¼ teaspoon salt, plus more for sprinkling

6 tablespoons unsalted butter, at room temperature, plus more for the pan

½ cup granulated sugar

½ cup firmly packed light brown sugar

2 large eggs, at room temperature

½ cup buttermilk, at room temperature

1 teaspoon pure vanilla extract

¾ cup mini semisweet chocolate chips

½ cup golden raisins

½ teaspoon grated orange zest

FROSTING

4 ounces cream cheese, cut into pieces, at room temperature

¼ cup (½ stick) unsalted butter, cut into pieces, at room temperature

Pinch of salt

3 ounces premium unsweetened chocolate, melted (see page 23) and cooled

½ teaspoon pure vanilla extract

½ teaspoon grated orange zest (optional)

About 1¾ cups sifted powdered sugar

About 2 tablespoons cream, half-and-half, or milk

TO MAKE THE CAKE: Preheat the oven to 350°F. Lightly butter the bottom and sides of a 9-inch round cake pan. Line the bottom of the pan with a round of parchment or waxed paper.

In a strainer, combine the zucchini and carrot and generously sprinkle with salt. Let the mixture drain for 30 minutes, then rinse and squeeze dry. There should be about 1½ cups. In a small bowl, whisk the flour, the unsweetened and Dutch-process cocoas, baking soda, and ¼ teaspoon salt until well blended. Set the zucchini mixture and flour mixture aside.

In a bowl, with a stand or hand mixer set on low speed, beat the 6 tablespoons butter until creamy. Add the granulated and brown sugars and beat until light and fluffy. Beat in the eggs, one at a time, until fully blended, scraping down the sides and bottom of the bowl as necessary. Beat in the buttermilk and vanilla until blended. Using a rubber spatula or wooden spoon, fold in the dry ingredients, followed by the grated zucchini mixture, chocolate chips, raisins, and orange zest. Stop when the ingredients are just blended. Scrape the batter into the prepared pan and spread evenly. Bake until the cake is springy to the touch and a tester inserted in the center comes out with a few moist crumbs clinging to it, about 45 minutes.

Transfer to a wire rack for at least 15 minutes. Gently loosen the edges with a thin knife before unmolding, right side up, onto a wire rack. Let cool completely, then carefully peel off the parchment before dusting with powdered sugar (see headnote) or frosting.

TO MAKE THE FROSTING: Make sure the cream cheese and butter are not too warm, or the frosting will be too soft. In a stand mixer or with a hand mixer set on medium-low speed, beat the cream cheese, butter, and salt until smooth and creamy. Beat in the chocolate, vanilla, and orange zest, if desired, until blended. Gradually beat in the powdered sugar and the cream and continue to beat until the frosting reaches a spreading consistency.

continued

TO ASSEMBLE THE CAKE: Place a dollop of frosting in the middle of a cake stand. Place the cake on the stand, top side up, and, using an off-set spatula, spread the top and the sides of the cake with the frosting. The cake can be frosted 1 day ahead and kept in a cake keeper at cool (60° to 70°F) room temperature.

VARIATION

For **Aunt Trudy's Dress-Up Chocolate Cake**, follow the main recipe, substituting Red-Wine Raisins (page 57) for the golden raisins and Chocolate–Grand Marnier Ganache (recipe follows) for the chocolate–cream cheese frosting.

CHOCOLATE–GRAND MARNIER GANACHE

6 ounces premium dark chocolate, chopped

¼ cup heavy (whipping) cream

1 tablespoon Grand Marnier or other orange-flavored liqueur

1 to 2 teaspoons freshly grated orange zest

Place the chocolate and cream in a medium heatproof bowl and set in a wide pan or skillet of hot water. Set aside for 5 minutes, stirring 4 or 5 times, and let the chocolate melt completely. Stir until smooth. Stir in the Grand Marnier and 1 teaspoon zest. Taste and adjust the seasoning with more zest if needed. Let stand to thicken to a spreading consistency, or refrigerate until slightly chilled, checking frequently.

To glaze, set the cake on a serving plate. Pour the entire glaze over the center of the cake. Using an offset metal spatula, spread the ganache over the top of the cake so it runs down the sides. Work quickly, using as few strokes as possible. Don't worry about puddles; think of them as more chocolate per serving. Serve immediately or store at cool (60° to 70°F) room temperature.

state fair
CHOCOLATE
LAYER CAKE

Serves
10 TO 12
MAKES ONE
9-INCH CAKE

MY FRIEND JEANNE SUBOTNICK GAVE ME THIS SOUR CREAM
and chocolate layer-cake recipe, which is coupled with the lingering memory of
a prize-winning cake I tasted years ago at the Oregon State Fair. In Oregon, you
wouldn't be caught dead bringing a cake to the Salem fair unless it's at least four
layers tall. (Otherwise, Judge Gerry Frank wouldn't give it a second look.) I've
taken the liberty of adapting the recipe to make a two-layer version of the cake.

CAKE

2 cups cake flour

2 teaspoons baking soda

½ teaspoon salt

½ cup (1 stick) unsalted butter, at
   room temperature, plus more for
   the pans

1¼ cups granulated sugar

1 cup firmly packed light brown sugar

3 large eggs, at room temperature

4 ounces premium dark chocolate,
   melted (see page 23) and cooled

2 teaspoons pure vanilla extract

1 cup sour cream

1 cup hot, strong coffee

FROSTING

3⅔ cups powdered sugar

2 tablespoons premium unsweetened
   Dutch-process cocoa powder

Pinch of salt

½ cup (1 stick) unsalted butter, cut
   into pieces, at room temperature

5 ounces unsweetened chocolate,
   melted and cooled

2 teaspoons pure vanilla extract

About 6 tablespoons milk or heavy
   (whipping) cream, at room
   temperature or slightly warm

TO MAKE THE CAKE: Preheat the oven to 350°F. Lightly butter the
bottom and sides of two 9-inch round cake pans. Line the bottom of
each pan with a round of parchment or waxed paper.

continued

In a medium bowl, whisk the flour, baking soda, and salt until well blended. Set aside.

With a stand or hand mixer set on medium speed, beat the ½ cup butter until creamy. Add the granulated and brown sugars and beat until light and fluffy, about 3 minutes. Beat in the eggs, one at a time, until fully blended, scraping down the sides and bottom of the bowl. On low speed, beat in the melted chocolate and vanilla. Alternately blend the dry ingredients and the sour cream in increments until all is combined, again scraping down the bowl as necessary. With the mixer still on low speed, slowly pour in the coffee and beat until blended.

Divide the batter between the prepared pans, and spread evenly. Gently rotate the pans to settle and level the batter. Bake until the cakes are springy to the touch and a tester inserted in the center comes out with a few moist crumbs clinging to it, 30 to 35 minutes. Let the layers cool on a wire rack in their pans for at least 15 minutes. Gently loosen the edges with a thin knife before inverting the layers onto the racks. Let the cakes cool thoroughly, about 2 hours, before carefully peeling off the parchment to frost them.

TO MAKE THE FROSTING: Sift the powdered sugar, cocoa, and salt into the bowl of a stand mixer. Add the butter. With the mixer set on low speed, slowly add the melted chocolate and vanilla. Slowly add the milk and continue beating until the frosting reaches spreading consistency, 1 to 2 minutes. Finish by increasing the speed to medium-high for 30 seconds.

TO ASSEMBLE THE CAKE: Place a dollop of frosting in the middle of a cake stand. Place 1 layer on the stand, top side up, and, using an offset spatula, spread 1 cup frosting evenly over the top. Place the remaining layer on top, bottom side up, and brush off any large, loose crumbs. Spread a thin layer of frosting over the top and sides of the cake to seal in the remaining crumbs. Refrigerate the cake for 1 hour, leaving the remaining frosting at room temperature. Spread the remaining frosting evenly over the top and sides of the cake. The cake can be frosted 1 day ahead and kept in a cake keeper at cool (60° to 70°F) room temperature until ready to serve.

one-bite-to-heaven
CHOCOLATE YEAST CAKE

serves
10

MAKES ONE
10-INCH TUBE CAKE

I FOUND THIS UNUSUAL CHOCOLATE CAKE IN A RECIPE box that belonged to my husband's mother, Mary Perry. She was a terrific home baker. When she died, I inherited her red-tin encyclopedia of hand-written family favorites. This particular recipe caught my eye when I was testing recipes for this book. With my first bite, I knew I had to include it. The cake is firm and sturdy and goes beautifully with hot coffee.

You could top this cake with chocolate sauce or a flavored sugar syrup (rum would be a good candidate for flavoring) and serve it with whipped cream, but I think it's best plain and simple.

4 to 4½ teaspoons (2 packages) active
    dry yeast
¼ cup warm (110° to 115°F) water
¾ cup warm (110° to 115°F) whole milk
3 cups sifted all-purpose flour, divided
½ cup (1 stick) unsalted butter, at
    room temperature

2 cups granulated sugar
3 large eggs, at room temperature
½ teaspoon pure vanilla extract
1 teaspoon baking soda
½ teaspoon salt
6 ounces premium dark chocolate,
    melted (see page 23)

In a medium bowl, sprinkle the yeast over the warm water and stir to blend. Let sit until foamy, about 5 minutes. Stir and mix in the milk and 1½ cups of the flour until smooth. Cover and let rise in a warm place until light and spongy, about 30 minutes.

With a stand or hand mixer set on medium speed, beat the butter and sugar until light and fluffy. Beat in the eggs, one at a time, until fully blended, scraping down the sides and bottom of the bowl as necessary. Add the yeast mixture and vanilla and beat until just blended.

In another bowl, whisk the remaining 1½ cups flour, the baking soda, and salt until blended. Add the flour mixture to the yeast mixture, alternating with the melted chocolate, and beat until well blended and smooth. Scrape down the sides and bottom of the bowl again.

Generously butter a 10-inch tube pan. Scrape the dough into the prepared pan, cover with plastic wrap, and let rise in a warm place until light and bubbly, about 1 hour. After 40 minutes, preheat the oven to 350°F. Uncover the dough and bake until a tester inserted in the center comes out clean and the cake begins to pull away from the sides of the pan, about 50 minutes. Let the cake cool on a wire rack in the pan for at least 20 minutes. Gently loosen the edges with a thin knife before inverting onto the rack. Serve warm or at room temperature.

papa haydn's
CHOCOLATE
GÂTEAU

serves
10 TO 12
MAKES
ONE CAKE

EVELYN FRANZ IS A GENIUS WHEN IT COMES TO CREATING
chocolate desserts. For nearly thirty years, she has been the mastermind
behind the elegant and delicious desserts at Papa Haydn's, a restaurant she
co-founded in Portland, Oregon. She first tasted this cake in London at the
River Café. They called it "chocolate nemesis," but for her, it was love at first
bite. Luckily for us, when she returned home, Evelyn developed a recipe for
her own rendition.

12 ounces premium dark chocolate,
chopped

⅓ cup hot or warm espresso or strong
coffee

½ cup heavy (whipping) cream

4 large eggs, at room temperature

2 large egg yolks, at room
temperature

½ cup granulated sugar

Pinch of salt

Lightly sweetened and whipped heavy
cream for serving

Preheat the oven to 350°F. Lightly butter the bottom and sides of an
8-inch round cake pan. Line the bottom with a round of parchment
or waxed paper. (If using a springform pan, wrap the outside with
aluminum foil to avoid leaking.) Prepare a water bath by placing a terry-
cloth washcloth in the bottom of a roasting or similar-style pan. (This
prevents the pan from sliding, insulates the bottom, and helps prevent
overcooking.)

Place the chocolate and espresso in a large heatproof bowl and set
in a wide pan or skillet of hot water. Set aside for 5 minutes, stirring

continued

4 or 5 times, and let the chocolate melt completely. Stir until smooth and keep warm. Using a hand mixer with clean beaters, whip the cream until soft peaks form. Set aside.

Remove the bowl of a stand mixer and place it in a hot (150° to 155°F) water bath. Add the eggs, yolks, sugar, and salt and, with a hand-held mixer, beat until the mixture is warm and the sugar is dissolved, 2 to 3 minutes. Reattach the bowl to the stand mixer fitted with the whisk attachment and whisk the mixture on high speed until light and fluffy, 2 to 3 minutes.

Alternately fold one-third of the egg mixture and one-third of the whipped cream into the chocolate mixture until all is combined. Pour the batter into the prepared cake pan. Place the pan on the washcloth in the roasting pan and fill the roasting pan with enough hot water to reach halfway up the sides of the cake pan. Bake until the top of the cake is set, 80 to 90 minutes. Remove the cake from the water bath and let cool on a wire rack for 30 minutes. Gently loosen the edges with a thin knife before inverting onto the rack. To serve, carefully remove the parchment and refrigerate until cool, at least 2 hours. Slice into thin wedges and serve with the sweetened whipped cream.

CHOCOLATE GINGERBREAD
WITH CACAO-NIB
whipped cream

Serves
8
MAKES ONE 9-INCH
ROUND CAKE

THIS IS THE DESSERT TO MAKE WHEN YOU WANT YOUR
kitchen to smell heavenly and your guests to feel at home. The cake is simple
but wonderful, with intriguing tastes and the texture of fresh ginger flecks
interlaced with premium chocolate. It will become one of your favorites, especially when you serve it warm from the oven with a lofty helping of cacao-nib
whipped cream.

WHIPPED CREAM

2 cups heavy (whipping) cream

¼ cup premium cacao nibs, chopped
into small bits

2 tablespoons granulated sugar, or
more to taste

Pinch of salt

GINGERBREAD

2 ounces premium dark chocolate,
chopped

½ cup (1 stick) unsalted butter, cut
into pieces, plus more for the pan

1½ cups all-purpose flour, plus more
for the pan

⅓ cup granulated sugar

3 tablespoons premium unsweetened
cocoa powder, plus more for dusting
(optional)

¾ teaspoon ground allspice

½ teaspoon baking soda

¼ teaspoon salt

3 tablespoons peeled and minced
fresh ginger (about 1½ ounces
whole)

⅓ cup firmly packed dark brown
sugar

⅓ cup dark honey, at room
temperature or slightly warm

1 large egg, at room temperature,
lightly beaten

⅓ cup buttermilk, at room
temperature

Powdered sugar for dusting
(optional)

continued

TO MAKE THE WHIPPED CREAM: At least 6 hours before serving, in a small saucepan over medium-high heat, combine the cream, nibs, sugar, and salt and bring the mixture to a gentle boil. Remove from the heat, cover, and steep for 30 minutes. Strain the cream through a fine-mesh sieve and discard the nibs. Cover and refrigerate the cream for at least 5 hours or up to 2 days. When ready to use, whip the chilled cream until soft peaks form.

TO MAKE THE GINGERBREAD: Preheat the oven to 325°F. Lightly butter and flour (or dust with cocoa) a 9-inch round cake pan. Place the chocolate and ½ cup butter in a large heatproof bowl and set in a wide pan or skillet of hot water. Set aside for 5 minutes, stirring 4 or 5 times, and let the chocolate melt completely. Stir occasionally until the mixture is smooth and cools slightly.

In a medium bowl, whisk the 1½ cups flour, the sugar, cocoa, allspice, baking soda, and salt until well blended. Stir in the minced ginger until coated and evenly distributed. Add the brown sugar and honey to the bowl containing the cooled chocolate mixture and stir until blended. Add the beaten egg and mix until blended. Mix in the buttermilk, scraping down the sides and bottom of the bowl as necessary. Add the dry ingredients in several additions and beat until just blended and smooth. Do not overmix.

Scrape the batter into the prepared pan and spread evenly. Gently rotate the pan to settle and level the batter. Bake until the gingerbread is springy to the touch and a tester inserted in the center comes out with a few moist crumbs clinging to it, about 40 minutes. Let the ginger-bread cool on a wire rack for 20 minutes. Gently loosen the edges with a thin knife before inverting it onto the rack. Dust with powdered sugar, if desired. Serve warm with a good portion of the whipped cream.

lamington CAKES

makes
24
SMALL (2-INCH) CAKES

THESE INDIVIDUAL COCONUT-CHOCOLATE LAYER CAKES, laced with raspberry, are one of my favorite desserts. Every bite offers a tantalizing combination of flavors and textures. Similar to large petit fours—but much better—they are ideal for parties or for any celebration where cake is in order (which covers just about every occasion). Lamingtons take a bit of planning and should be assembled the day before you serve them so the flavors have time to meld.

Are you wondering what, or who, is a Lamington? These small cakes were supposedly named after Baron Lamington, a popular governor of Queensland from 1896 to 1901. Some think the word was slang for the homburg hat he liked to wear. Today, Lamington Cakes are still popular as an Australian afternoon teacake.

CAKE

1 cup (2 sticks) unsalted butter, cut into pieces, plus more for the pan

3/4 cup water

2 ounces premium unsweetened chocolate, chopped

1 teaspoon instant coffee, decaffeinated or regular

2 cups granulated sugar

1 1/2 cups all-purpose flour

1/2 cup premium unsweetened cocoa powder

1 teaspoon baking soda

1/2 teaspoon salt

1/2 cup buttermilk, at room temperature

2 large eggs, at room temperature, lightly beaten

1 1/2 teaspoons pure vanilla extract

1 cup raspberry jam, strained to remove seeds, divided

GLAZE

2 cups sifted powdered sugar

3/4 cup hot water

1/2 cup premium unsweetened cocoa powder

3 tablespoons unsalted butter

3 to 3 1/2 cups unsweetened, shredded dried coconut such as Bob's Red Mill

TO MAKE THE CAKE: Preheat the oven to 375°F. Lightly butter a 13-by-9-by-2-inch straight-sided metal baking pan. To make removing the finished cake easy, line the pan lengthwise with a 17-by-8-inch sheet of parchment paper or aluminum foil (shiny side up) and use the overhang as handles.

In a medium saucepan over medium heat, combine the 1 cup butter, the water, chocolate, and instant coffee and cook, stirring, until the chocolate is melted and the mixture is smooth. Remove from the heat. In a large bowl, whisk the sugar, flour, cocoa, baking soda, and salt until well blended. Gradually whisk the lukewarm chocolate mixture into the dry ingredients until smooth. Beat in the buttermilk, eggs, and vanilla until blended and smooth, scraping down the sides and bottom of the bowl as necessary.

Scrape the batter into the prepared pan. Gently tap the pan several times on a counter to settle the batter. Bake until the cake is springy to the touch and a tester inserted in the center comes out just clean or with a few moist crumbs clinging to it, about 35 minutes. Transfer to a wire rack to cool completely.

Using the parchment handles, lift the cake from the pan and place on a work surface. Cut the cake into quarters, place on a large baking sheet lined with waxed paper, and freeze for 1 hour. Remove 1 cake quarter from the freezer. Using a serrated bread knife, stand the cake on edge and cut in half widthwise. Lay the 2 halves side by side, cut side up, and spread one half with ¼ cup of the raspberry jam. Using a stiff spatula, place the other half on top and return it to the baking sheet. Repeat with the remaining 3 cake quarters. Freeze the 4 quarters for 2 to 3 hours longer.

Remove the cakes from the freezer. Using the serrated bread knife, trim away any rough edges. Cut each quarter into 6 squares and place them back on the tray. Return to the freezer while you make the glaze.

continued

TO MAKE THE GLAZE: In a medium saucepan over low heat, combine the powdered sugar, hot water, cocoa, and butter. Heat, stirring, until the mixture is blended and smooth.

TO ASSEMBLE THE CAKES: Place the saucepan containing the glaze on a clean counter top. Arrange the pan of cakes on one side of the saucepan, a bowl containing 3 cups of the coconut in front of the saucepan, and, on the other side, 2 wire racks set on another baking sheet. Holding each cake on a fork, dip it into the glaze, draining any excess back into the saucepan. Using the fork, roll the cake in the coconut to coat. Place the finished cake on a rack and repeat with the remaining cakes, replenishing the coconut as needed. Use an inverted shallow roasting pan to cover the cakes until serving time. These cakes taste best when allowed to rest 6 to 8 hours or overnight.

wedding cupcakes with WEDDING-PARTY FROSTINGS

makes
12
CUPCAKES

FOR BETTER OR FOR BEST, AT YOUR NEXT WEDDING, SKIP the high-rise, frou-frou fondant cake and go for tiers of delicious, dark chocolate cupcakes decorated with an array of great-tasting frostings. This is a cake your guests will actually eat and remember . . . plus, there'll be no fighting over the largest slice.

A note on the party cups called for in this recipe, and a word of praise for Cheryl Porro: Cheryl is a software engineer by day and the author of www.cupcakeblog.com. I came upon her Web site and was immediately taken by her cupcake liners, which she explains are Wilton's standard-size "Nut & Party" cups. Check them out in Sources (page 192) or on Cheryl's site. They're nifty.

Adding the small amount of Dutch-process cocoa powder here gives the cupcakes a darker color. If you don't have any, it's fine to leave it out.

⅓ cup premium unsweetened cocoa powder

1 tablespoon premium unsweetened Dutch-process cocoa powder (optional)

½ cup very hot coffee

1 cup all-purpose flour

½ teaspoon baking soda

Pinch of salt

6 tablespoons (¾ stick) unsalted butter, at room temperature

⅔ cup granulated sugar

1 large egg, at room temperature

1 large egg yolk, at room temperature

½ teaspoon pure vanilla extract

Wedding-Party Frostings (page 85–89)

Preheat the oven to 350°F. Arrange twelve 3¼-ounce, 2-inch paper party cups on a large, heavy-duty baking sheet or add liners to a standard 12-cup muffin tin.

In a small bowl, combine the unsweetened cocoa, the Dutch-process cocoa (if desired) and the coffee. Stir until well blended and let rest for 5 minutes. In another small bowl, whisk the flour, baking soda, and salt until well blended. Set aside.

In a stand mixer or with a hand mixer set on low speed, beat the butter and sugar until light and fluffy. Beat in the whole egg and egg yolk, one at a time, until fully blended, scraping down the sides and bottom of the bowl as necessary. Beat in the vanilla until blended.

Stir the coffee-cocoa mixture again and beat it into the butter mixture in increments, alternating with the dry ingredients, until just blended and smooth. Scrape down the bowl again. Divide the batter equally between the cups, filling each ¾ full. Bake until a tester inserted in the middle comes out just clean, 20 to 24 minutes. Do not overbake. Transfer to a wire rack to cool completely before frosting.

• •

BACHELOR'S PERFECT PEANUT BUTTER

makes about
2 ¹/₄
CUPS

6 ounces cream cheese, at room temperature, cut into pieces
⅓ cup unsalted butter, at room temperature, cut into pieces
¼ cup smooth peanut butter

¼ teaspoon pure vanilla extract
2 cups sifted powdered sugar
1 cup chopped peanuts, plain, dry-roasted, or lightly salted (optional)

Make sure the cream cheese and butter are not too warm or the frosting will be too soft. In a stand mixer set on low speed, combine the cream cheese, butter, peanut butter, and vanilla. Slowly add the powdered sugar and mix until smooth. To finish, increase the speed to medium-high for 30 seconds. To frost, top each cupcake with a generous amount of frosting. To decorate, sprinkle with the chopped peanuts, if desired, and press them lightly into the frosting. Serve at room temperature.

continued

WEDDING-PARTY FROSTINGS

THE-BRIDE-WORE-WHITE COCONUT

makes about
2 ⅓
CUPS

8 ounces cream cheese, at room
temperature, cut into pieces

½ cup (1 stick) unsalted butter, at
room temperature, cut into pieces

½ teaspoon pure vanilla extract

Scant ¼ teaspoon pure almond extract

2 cups sifted powdered sugar

4 ounces sweetened shredded coconut

Make sure the cream cheese and butter are not too warm or the frosting will be too soft. In a stand mixer set on low speed, combine the cream cheese, butter, vanilla, and almond extract. Slowly add the powdered sugar and mix until smooth. To finish, increase the speed to medium-high for 30 seconds. To frost, top each cupcake with a generous amount of frosting. To decorate, sprinkle with the coconut and press it lightly into the frosting. Serve at room temperature.

VARIATION:

For **Pretty-in-Pink Flower Girl** frosting, follow the main recipe. After blending all the ingredients, mix in a drop of red or pink food coloring. Make sure to mix each drop thoroughly before adding another. Proceed as directed, substituting decorative sugars or sprinkles for the shredded coconut.

continued

BEST MAN'S CHOCOLATE TEQUILA

makes about

2 ¹/₄

CUPS

1½ bars (3 ounces) Dagoba Xocolatl (74%) (chilies/nibs) or other premium dark chocolate, chopped

6 tablespoons unsalted butter, cut into pieces

Pinch of salt

3 cups sifted powdered sugar

3 tablespoons milk

2 tablespoons good-quality tequila, or more to taste

Place the chocolate, butter, and salt in a medium heatproof bowl and set in a wide pan or skillet of hot water. Set aside for 5 minutes, stirring 4 or 5 times, and let the chocolate melt completely. Stir until smooth.

In a stand mixer or with a hand mixer set on low speed, beat the powdered sugar, milk, and tequila. Slowly add the melted chocolate mixture and beat until smooth. Taste and adjust the flavor by adding more tequila to taste. If the mixture is slightly runny, let it cool and it will stiffen. Spread or mound over the cooled cupcakes and let set.

WEDDING PLANNER'S CARAMEL CHOCOLATE

makes about

2 ³/₄

CUPS

1 recipe Caramel Sauce (page 159), chilled

½ recipe "It's My Party" Birthday Cake chocolate frosting (page 62)

Warm the caramel sauce slightly so it is spreadable (it will still be cooler than room temperature). To frost the cupcakes, have both toppings within easy reach. Using a 1-tablespoon measuring spoon, fill it a little more than halfway with caramel sauce, then pour the sauce on the center of a cupcake. Using a small knife or spatula, spread the caramel over most of the top. It's fine if a bit goes over the edge. Using an offset spatula, spread a layer of the chocolate filling on top of the caramel. Repeat to frost all the cupcakes and let set at cool (60° to 70°F) room temperature. If desired, you can refrigerate the cupcakes for 10 minutes to set the frosting faster.

TIL-DEATH-DO-US-PART CHOCOLATE

makes about

2 ¹/₃

CUPS

3 ½ ounces premium unsweetened chocolate, chopped

7 tablespoons unsalted butter, cut into pieces

Pinch of salt

3 ½ cups sifted powdered sugar

5 tablespoons milk or cream

Place the chocolate, butter, and salt in a medium heatproof bowl and set in a wide pan or skillet of hot water. Set aside for 5 minutes, stirring 4 or 5 times, and let the chocolate melt completely. Stir until smooth.

In a stand mixer or with a hand mixer set on low speed, beat the powdered sugar and milk. Slowly add the melted chocolate mixture and beat until smooth. If the mixture is slightly runny, let it cool and it will stiffen. Spread or mound over the cooled cupcakes and let set.

six tall CHOCOLATE–SOUR CREAM CUPCAKES

makes 6 TALL CUPCAKES

SOMETIMES BIGGER REALLY IS BETTER. IT HAPPENED quite by accident: I had buttered the popover pan instead of the cupcake tin. Dividing the batter evenly among the popover cups, I popped the pan in the oven. The delightful result was 6 big, crusty, mushroom-shaped cupcakes. If you fill the cups with a lighter hand, you'll be rewarded with a taller, equally delicious version.

CUPCAKES

¾ cup all-purpose flour

3 tablespoons premium unsweetened Dutch-process cocoa powder

½ teaspoon baking soda

Large pinch of salt

¼ cup unsalted butter, at room temperature, plus more for the pan

¾ cup firmly packed light brown sugar

1 ounce premium dark chocolate, melted (see page 23)

1 large egg, at room temperature

½ teaspoon pure vanilla extract

½ cup sour cream

FROSTING

½ cup sour cream

½ cup powdered sugar

1 bar (3.5 ounces) premium dark chocolate, melted and cooled to lukewarm

TO MAKE THE CUPCAKES: Preheat the oven to 350°F. *Generously* butter each cup of a 6-cup popover pan.

In a bowl, whisk the flour, Dutch-process cocoa powder, baking soda, and salt until well blended. Set aside.

In a stand mixer or with a hand mixer set on low speed, beat the ¼ cup butter until creamy. Add the sugar and beat on medium speed until light and fluffy. Alternately add the melted chocolate, then the egg and vanilla, blending well after each addition. Mix in the sour cream.

For tall cupcakes, fill each cup about two-thirds full (about 6 tablespoons of batter); some batter will be left over. For tall, mushroom-capped cupcakes, divide the batter equally between the cups (about 8 tablespoons of batter each). Bake until a long tester or skewer inserted in the center comes out with a few moist crumbs clinging to it, about 20 minutes. Do not overbake. Let the cupcakes cool in the pan on a wire rack for 25 minutes. Then, to remove them, loosen the caps by running a thin knife under them, then turn the pan over and gently tap it on the counter. Let cool completely on the rack.

TO MAKE THE FROSTING: In a medium bowl, mix or whisk the sour cream and powdered sugar until blended. Stir in the chocolate until blended and smooth. Top the cupcakes with a thick and even layer of frosting.

VARIATIONS

Our kids came up with this one. For **Six Moms and Their Kids' Cupcakes**, follow the main recipe for the mushroom-capped cupcakes. After the cupcakes have cooled, cut off the tops or caps for the kids and reserve the lower portions for the moms. Frost both.

For **A Dozen Little Ones**, follow the main recipe using twelve 3¼-ounce, 2-inch paper party cups (available from Wilton Industries Inc.; see Sources, page 192) on a baking sheet or a standard 12-cup muffin tin. Reduce the baking time to 15 minutes.

DEEP CHOCOLATE PIES

tarts, and a

CHEESECAKE

SOME MORE S'MORE PIE, PLEASE
95

Marmalade and Bittersweet Chocolate Tarts
97

Wednesday Wild's Wintertime Chocolate-Caramel Tart
100

a little chocolate cheesecake with mocha affogato
104

some more S'MORE PIE, PLEASE

Serves 6

MAKES ONE
9-INCH TART

WHO CAN RESIST THE COMBINATION OF DARK CHOCOLATE, crunchy graham crackers, and warm, melt-in-your-mouth marshmallows, especially when you can dispense with hauling wood for the campfire? If you're on the lookout for a plate-and-fork way to enjoy one of the most revered trinity of treats, this scrumptious, deeply homey pie is for you.

CRUST
1⅓ cups graham cracker crumbs
⅓ cup granulated sugar
5 tablespoons unsalted butter, melted

2 tablespoons unsalted butter, cut into pieces
Pinch of salt
½ teaspoon pure vanilla extract

FILLING
5 ounces premium dark chocolate, chopped
½ cup whole milk

TOPPING
18 large, fresh purchased marshmallows

TO MAKE THE CRUST: Preheat the oven to 350°F. In a medium bowl, mix the graham cracker crumbs, sugar, and melted butter until well blended and crumbly. Transfer the mixture to a 9-inch freezer-to-oven pie pan and lightly press onto the bottom of the pan. Bake until set and fragrant, 12 to 15 minutes. Transfer to a wire rack and let cool to room temperature.

TO MAKE THE FILLING: Place the chocolate in a medium heatproof bowl. In a small saucepan over medium heat, heat the milk and butter

continued

until the butter is melted and small bubbles form around the edges of the pan. Stir to combine. Pour the hot milk mixture over the chocolate. Let stand for several minutes, then stir until the chocolate is melted and the mixture is smooth. Stir in the salt and vanilla until blended. Let cool completely. Pour into the crust and refrigerate until well chilled, at least 4 hours, or preferably overnight.

TO MAKE THE TOPPING: Heat the oven broiler to low. Cut each marshmallow in half crosswise and arrange the halves, cut side down, to cover the top of the pie. Place the pie on the lowest rack in the oven until the marshmallows toast. Watch carefully; once they start to brown, they toast quickly. Serve while the marshmallows are still warm.

marmalade and
BITTERSWEET CHOCOLATE
TARTS

makes
8
4-INCH
TARTS

THESE DARK, RICH, VELVETY TARTS ARE IDEAL AS A SIMPLE
dessert with coffee or tea, or an end-of-dinner flourish with a fine dessert
wine. If you like, you can garnish the tarts with grated orange zest. A small
scoop of orange sorbet also complements the flavors.

CRUST
1½ cups all-purpose flour
3 tablespoons granulated sugar
1½ teaspoons grated orange zest
Pinch of salt
½ cup plus 1 tablespoon unsalted butter,
    frozen and cut into small pieces
2 to 4 tablespoons ice water

FILLING
¾ cup premium orange marmalade
9 ounces premium dark chocolate,
    chopped
¾ cup heavy (whipping) cream

Finely grated orange zest or candied
    orange peel for garnish (optional)

TO MAKE THE CRUST: In a medium bowl, whisk the flour, sugar, orange
zest, and salt until well blended. Add the butter. Using your fingers or
a pastry blender, work the butter into the flour mixture until crumbly
and some pea-sized pieces of butter remain. If time permits, refrigerate the flour mixture for 30 minutes.

Drizzle the ice water over the flour mixture, 1 tablespoon at a time,
mixing until all the flour is moistened and the pastry just clears the
side of the bowl (add an additional 1 to 2 teaspoons water if needed).
Using lightly floured hands, gather the dough into a ball. Shape into a
disk, wrap in plastic wrap, and refrigerate for 1 hour.

continued

Remove the dough from the refrigerator and cut it into 8 wedges, then reshape each wedge into a disk without reworking the dough (if needed, let it sit out to soften slightly for easier handling). Roll each disk out to a 5- to 6-inch circle on a pastry cloth or lightly floured board with a cloth-covered rolling pin or between 2 sheets of heavy-duty plastic wrap. Transfer a circle of the dough to a 4-inch tart pan, easing it into place. Trim the overhanging pastry along the pan's edge. Repeat with remaining disks. Refrigerate for 30 minutes to 1 hour.

Preheat the oven to 375°F. Prick the bottom of each crust with a fork, line with a circle of parchment or aluminum foil, and fill to the top with pie weights or dried beans. Bake in the center of the oven until the edges begin to turn golden, 15 to 20 minutes. Remove the weights and parchment and bake until the crusts are golden, 8 to 10 minutes more. Remove from the oven and transfer to a wire rack to cool.

TO MAKE THE FILLING: In a small saucepan, warm the marmalade until it is warm to the touch and slightly runny, and strain it through a sieve, discarding any pulp. Brush the bottom of each tart shell with some strained marmalade.

Place the chocolate in a medium bowl. In a small saucepan over medium heat, heat the cream and 2 tablespoons of the marmalade until small bubbles form around the edges of the pan. Pour the hot cream over the chocolate. Let stand for 3 to 4 minutes, then whisk until the mixture is smooth. Evenly divide the chocolate mixture between the tart shells. Allow the tart filling to set at cool (60° to 70°F) room temperature for at least 2 hours before serving. To serve, add a dollop of the remaining marmalade in the center of each tart and garnish each tart with finely grated orange zest or candied orange peel, if desired.

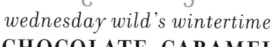

wednesday wild's wintertime
CHOCOLATE-CARAMEL
TART

Serves

8

MAKES ONE
11-INCH TART

HERE'S A TASTY TONGUE TWISTER: PORTLAND'S PALEY'S

Place pastry person Wednesday Wild welcomes wintry weather with this tempting tart.

To accompany the tart, Wednesday often serves an Earl Grey ice cream, with the signature flavor of citrus bergamot complementing the tart's caramel-almond filling and dark chocolate ganache. Another charming choice would be Cacao-Nib Whipped Cream (page 77).

CRUST
½ cup premium dark chocolate, chopped
2 tablespoons unsalted butter, cut into pieces
2 cups finely ground chocolate-wafer cookie crumbs made from store-bought cookies

FILLING
1 large egg
1 large egg yolk
2 teaspoons pure vanilla extract
Pinch of salt

1½ cups granulated sugar
½ cup water
1¼ cups heavy (whipping) cream, hot
2 cups whole toasted almonds

GANACHE
6 ounces premium dark chocolate, chopped
¾ cup heavy (whipped) cream
Pinch of salt
Earl Grey Ice Cream (page 102), Cacao-Nib Whipped Cream (page 77), or lightly sweetened, softly whipped cream for serving

TO MAKE THE CRUST: Preheat the oven to 375°F. Lightly coat an 11-inch tart pan with cooking spray. Place the chocolate and butter in a small saucepan and set in a wide pan or skillet of hot water. Set aside for 5 minutes, stirring 4 or 5 times, and let the chocolate melt completely.

Stir until smooth. In a medium bowl, combine the cookie crumbs and chocolate mixture until well blended. Transfer the mixture to the prepared tart pan and press the mixture onto the sides and bottom of the pan. Bake until set, lightly toasted, and smelling of chocolate, 10 to 15 minutes. Transfer to a wire rack and let cool to room temperature.

TO MAKE THE FILLING: Preheat the oven to 325°F. Place a medium bowl in the freezer. In another medium bowl, whisk the egg, egg yolk, vanilla, and salt until combined.

In a small, heavy saucepan over medium heat, combine the sugar and water. Stir until the sugar dissolves, and let the mixture cook until it turns light caramel. Remove from the heat and slowly stir in the hot cream until blended. Watch out for spatters. Pour the caramel mixture into the bowl that has been chilling in the freezer. Add the almonds and continue to stir until the mixture cools. Slowly whisk the almond mixture into the egg mixture until blended. Pour the combined mixture into the prepared tart crust and bake until the filling bubbles slightly and the center is almost set, 30 to 40 minutes. Transfer to a wire rack and let cool completely.

TO MAKE THE GANACHE: Place the chocolate in a small bowl. In a small saucepan over medium heat, heat the cream and salt until small bubbles form around the edges of the pan. Pour the hot cream over the chocolate. Let stand for 3 to 4 minutes, then stir until the mixture is smooth. Spread the ganache over the cooled tart and refrigerate uncovered until the ganache is set, about 1 hour. Serve each chilled wedge with a small scoop of Earl Grey Ice Cream or whipped cream.

continued

EARL GREY ICE CREAM

makes about
1 ½
QUARTS ICE CREAM

3 cups heavy (whipping) cream

1 cup half-and-half

3 premium Earl Grey tea bags such as Tazo, Taylors of Harrogate, or Twinings

Pinch of salt

8 large egg yolks, at room temperature

½ cup granulated sugar

½ cup firmly packed light brown sugar

Pour the cream, half-and-half, tea bags, and salt into the top of a double boiler set over simmering water. Heat until small bubbles appear around the edges of the pan. Meanwhile, in a medium bowl, whisk the egg yolks and granulated and brown sugars until thick and smooth, 2 to 3 minutes. Gradually whisk ½ cup of the hot cream and Earl Grey mixture into the yolk mixture, then gradually whisk the yolk mixture into the double boiler. Cook over simmering water, stirring constantly, until the custard thickens, 5 to 7 minutes. To check for doneness, draw your finger through the custard on the back of the spoon; it should leave a trail. Remove from the heat and let cool to room temperature.

Strain the custard through a fine-mesh sieve, pressing the tea bags to release any liquid. Discard the tea bags. (At this point, you could serve the custard as a sauce. Its flavor will deepen when chilled.) Cover the custard and refrigerate at least 3 hours or up to 3 days. Stir the mixture, then pour it into an ice-cream maker. Freeze according to the manufacturer's instructions.

a little chocolate
CHEESECAKE WITH
MOCHA AFFOGATO

serves
6 TO 8
MAKES ONE 7-INCH
CHEESECAKE

CHOCOLATE CHEESECAKE IS ONE OF THOSE SPECIAL
desserts that usually come in two sizes: large and larger. I wanted a luscious cheese-cake for everyday celebrations, just the right size to enjoy with a few friends. I think I've found it. To make it even richer, I've topped it with an affogato (literally "drowned" in Italian) which is basically just espresso poured over the cheesecake.

CRUST
¾ cup graham cracker crumbs

1 tablespoon granulated sugar

1 tablespoon premium unsweetened cocoa powder

2 tablespoons unsalted butter, melted

FILLING
4 ounces premium dark chocolate, chopped

1 tablespoon premium unsweetened Dutch-process cocoa powder

1 tablespoon hot water

12 ounces cream cheese, at room temperature

⅔ cup granulated sugar

¼ cup sour cream

1 teaspoon pure vanilla extract

1 large egg, at room temperature, lightly beaten

TOPPING
¾ cup sour cream

¼ cup granulated sugar

¼ teaspoon pure vanilla extract

Drop of pure almond extract

MOCHA AFFOGATO
¼ cup granulated sugar

¼ cup water

2 tablespoons unsweetened Dutch-process cocoa powder

1 tablespoon plus 2 teaspoons instant espresso powder such as Medaglia d'Oro

Pinch of salt

TO MAKE THE CRUST: Cut a strip of parchment 1 inch wider than the height of a 7-inch springform pan. Line the inside of the pan with the paper, letting the excess extend above the pan's rim.

In a medium bowl, mix the cracker crumbs, sugar, and cocoa until blended. Mix in the butter until well blended and crumbly. Transfer the mixture to the prepared pan and press the mixture onto the bottom of the pan. Refrigerate the crust while making the filling.

TO MAKE THE FILLING: Preheat the oven to 350°F. Place the chocolate in a small heatproof bowl and set in a wide pan or skillet of hot water for 5 minutes, stirring 4 or 5 times. Let it melt completely. Stir until smooth. In another bowl, mix the cocoa and hot water to make a smooth paste.

In a stand mixer on medium-low speed, beat the cream cheese, sugar, sour cream, and vanilla until creamy and smooth, scraping down the sides and bottom of the bowl as necessary. Beat in the egg until blended. Stir in the melted chocolate and dissolved cocoa until well blended. Scrape the batter into the prepared pan and spread evenly. Bake in the center of the oven for 40 to 45 minutes. After removing the cheesecake from the oven, reduce the oven temperature to 300°F.

TO MAKE THE TOPPING: Meanwhile, in a small bowl, mix the sour cream, sugar, vanilla, and almond extract until well blended. Gently spread the topping over the cheesecake and bake for another 15 to 20 minutes to set the top layer. Transfer the cheesecake to a wire rack. Using a thin-bladed knife, loosen the parchment from the inside edge of the pan (this helps prevent the cheesecake from cracking as it cools). Let cool for 3 hours, then wrap in plastic wrap and refrigerate until cold and set, at least 6 hours or overnight.

To unmold, release the sides of the springform pan and peel off the parchment. Let the cheesecake stand at room temperature for 30 minutes.

TO MAKE THE MOCHA AFFOGATO: In a small saucepan over medium-high heat, combine the sugar and water and bring to a boil, stirring until the sugar dissolves. Remove from the heat and whisk in the cocoa, espresso powder, and salt until smooth.

To serve, place cheesecake slices on dessert plates, then drizzle a small amount of mocha affogato in a pattern on the plate. Any leftover cheesecake can be kept, covered in the refrigerator, up to 3 days.

CHOCOLATE PUDDINGS, CUSTARDS, *and a* SOUFFLÉ

Mom's Real Chocolate Pudding
109

VIN SANTO AND BRIOCHE CHOCOLATE BREAD PUDDING
111

Tea-Cup Chocolate Custard with Star Anise
114

VALRHONA DARK CHOCOLATE POTS DE CRÈME
116

Full-Tilt Dark Chocolate with Zabaglione
119

black and white soufflé
121

mom's real
CHOCOLATE
PUDDING

Serves
6

MY MOTHER'S CHOCOLATE PUDDING IS OUR FAMILY'S
favorite homey dessert. Made in a double boiler with flour as the thickener,
it's an old-fashioned pudding that's luscious and simple to make. All that's
required is a little time and patience.

You can use granulated or brown sugar; either works well. The granulated
sugar highlights the chocolate flavor, while the light or dark brown sugar adds
a subtle caramel accent.

3 cups evaporated milk
(see Note, page 110)

¾ cup granulated sugar or firmly
packed brown sugar

4 ounces premium unsweetened
chocolate, chopped

¼ cup plus 2 tablespoons all-purpose
flour

¼ teaspoon salt

1 large egg, at room temperature,
lightly beaten

1 teaspoon pure vanilla extract

Chocolate Curls for garnish
(optional; page 110)

First, have patience and don't try to hurry the process. In the top of
a double boiler, combine the milk, sugar, and chocolate and place
over simmering water. Cook, stirring occasionally, until the chocolate
melts, about 10 minutes. It will be light brown and speckled.

Meanwhile, in a small bowl, whisk the flour and salt until well
blended. Then, whisk ½ cup of the warm chocolate mixture into the
flour until blended and smooth. Slowly whisk the dry ingredients back
into the double-boiler mixture. Continue to cook until thickened,

continued

stirring occasionally at first and more frequently at the end, 12 to 17 minutes. The pudding will be a rich brown.

In a small bowl, slowly whisk ¾ cup of the hot pudding mixture into the beaten egg, then slowly add the egg mixture back into the double boiler, whisking constantly, for 2 minutes. Remove from the heat and stir in the vanilla. Pour into a single serving bowl, or divide among 6 dessert bowls and chill. A skin will develop on the surface (when I was a child, this was my favorite part). If you don't want the skin, cover the pudding surface with plastic wrap and refrigerate for 4 to 6 hours. If desired, garnish each serving with a chocolate curl.

NOTE

My mom always used evaporated milk in this recipe. Evaporated milk is basically whole milk with 60 percent of the water removed, giving it the consistency of heavy cream. It gives a slightly nutty flavor to choco-late desserts. This is the way I like it. If you prefer, you can substitute half-and-half, whole milk, or a combination of the two.

• •

CHOCOLATE CURLS

To make chocolate curls: begin with a chocolate block (you'll need a thick block, such as a Scharffen Berger 9.7-ounce home baking bar, to create large ribbonlike curls). Place the chocolate in a warm spot at room tem-perature to soften slightly, about 1 hour. Drag a sharp, serrated vegetable peeler in one motion down one side of the bar from top to bottom to create the curl.

vin santo and brioche
CHOCOLATE
BREAD PUDDING

Serves 4 to 6

THIS ENHANCED VERSION OF BREAD PUDDING IS A SEDUCTIVE
combination of buttery brioche, sweet Tuscan wine-infused custard, plump
golden raisins, and premium dark chocolate. The addictive finish of crushed
amaretti cookies and crème fraîche is not optional!

½ cup golden raisins

1 cup *vin santo* or other sweet dessert
wine

1 loaf brioche, *pandoro*, or semolina
bread, preferably a day or two old

4 large eggs, at room temperature

¼ cup granulated sugar, plus more for
dusting

¼ teaspoon salt

1¾ cups half-and-half

1 teaspoon pure vanilla extract

1 thin bar (4 ounces) premium dark
chocolate, broken into irregular
¾-inch pieces

4 to 6 crushed amaretti cookies such
as Amaretti di Saronno, for dusting

Powdered sugar for dusting

Crème fraîche for serving

In a small saucepan over medium heat, bring the raisins and *vin santo*
to a simmer. Simmer for 5 minutes, remove from the heat, cover, and
steep for 30 minutes. Let cool and strain, reserving both the raisins
and the *vin santo*.

Generously butter a large, 3-inch-deep oval casserole or baking
dish, and dust the inside with granulated sugar. Tap out the excess.
Slice off the ends of the brioche and discard them. Cut the loaf into
eight ½-inch slices. (If you're using fresh bread, lightly toast it.) Cut
the slices in half on the diagonal and arrange them in the dish by

continued

leaning each half-slice against its partner with its cut-side down. A pattern will emerge of exposed rounded tops on one side and exposed square-cornered bottoms on the other side. Scatter the raisins over the dish.

Meanwhile, beat the eggs in a medium bowl, whisk in the ¼ cup of sugar and the salt, and beat until well blended. Beat in the half-and-half, then stir in the vanilla and the reserved *vin santo.* Ladle or pour the custard over the brioche, spooning custard over any pieces of brioche that are still exposed. Cover and refrigerate overnight.

Remove the dish from the refrigerator 30 minutes before baking. Tilt the pan and spoon any remaining custard in the pan over the brioche. Preheat the oven to 325°F. Prepare a water bath by placing a terry-cloth washcloth in the bottom of a roasting or similar-style pan. (This prevents the pan from sliding, insulates the bottom, and helps prevent overcooking.)

Lay the chocolate pieces on the exposed pieces of brioche. Place the dish on the washcloth in the prepared roasting pan. Fill the roasting pan with enough hot water to reach halfway up the sides of the dish. Bake until the top of the pudding is golden and the custard is set, about 45 minutes. Remove the pudding from the water bath and transfer to a wire rack to cool for 10 minutes.

Before serving, sprinkle the bread pudding with the crushed amaretti and a dusting of powdered sugar. Accompany each portion with a dollop of crème fraîche. The pudding is best eaten within a day or two of baking. Any leftovers should be kept covered in the refrigerator.

VARIATION

For **Rustic-style Bread Pudding** (as seen in the facing photo), substitute an 8-by-8-inch square baking pan. Instead of cutting each slice in half on the diagonal, tear each slice in 3 to 6 pieces and distribute them evenly over the prepared pan. Scatter the raisins among the pieces, tossing lightly. Proceed as directed.

tea-cup
CHOCOLATE CUSTARD
WITH STAR ANISE

serves
6

THIS SIMPLE, YET SOPHISTICATED, DESSERT HAS ONLY A few ingredients, so it's important to use the best and the freshest you can buy. Go for a premium chocolate and buy a new jar of star anise to replace the one that's been lurking in your kitchen cabinet far too long.

4 ounces premium dark chocolate, chopped

2 cups half-and-half

⅓ cup granulated sugar

¼ cup whole star-anise pods (about 8 pods)

2 large eggs, at room temperature

Place the chocolate in a medium heatproof bowl.

In a medium saucepan over medium heat, heat the half-and-half, sugar, and star anise until small bubbles form around the edges of the pan and stir to combine. Remove from the heat, cover, and steep for 1 hour.

Preheat the oven to 300°F. Strain the half-and-half through a fine-mesh sieve and discard the star anise. Reheat the half-and-half until small bubbles form around the edge of the pan, and pour it over the chocolate. Let stand for 3 to 4 minutes, then whisk until the mixture is smooth.

In a small bowl, whisk the eggs until frothy. Slowly whisk ½ cup of the chocolate mixture into the eggs until blended. Then slowly whisk the egg mixture into the remaining hot-chocolate mixture. Strain the chocolate custard through a fine-mesh sieve into a 4-cup measuring cup. Divide among six ½-cup ovenproof, Asian-style porcelain tea cups (without handles) or porcelain ramekins. Place the cups in a 13-by-9-by-2-inch baking pan. Fill the roasting pan with enough hot water to reach halfway up the sides of the teacups. Bake the custards until set, about 55 minutes or until the center is slightly jiggly. Remove the pan from the oven; let the custards cool in water in pan. Remove the custards from the water bath and transfer to a wire rack to cool to room temperature. Transfer to the refrigerator to chill, covered, until 30 minutes before serving.

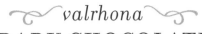

DARK CHOCOLATE
POTS DE CRÈME

Serves
6

THE TEXTURE OF THESE DEEP, DARK LITTLE POTS IS luxurious—it's like eating chocolate silk.

We thank chef Christopher Israel and Bruce Carey, owner of 23 Hoyt in Portland, Oregon, for this exquisite, lightly set, baked chocolate custard. At the restaurant, they use Valrhona Guanaja bittersweet chocolate, but feel free to use any premium dark chocolate with a flavor that delights you.

6 ounces Valrhona Guanaja chocolate (70%) or other premium dark chocolate (64% to 72%), chopped
1½ cups heavy (whipping) cream
1 cup whole milk

6 large egg yolks, at room temperature
½ cup plus 2 tablespoons granulated sugar

Place the chocolate in a medium heatproof bowl.

In a heavy, medium saucepan over medium heat, heat the cream and milk until small bubbles form around the edges of the pan.

Meanwhile, in a bowl, whisk the egg yolks and sugar until thick and smooth, about 3 minutes. Gradually whisk ½ cup of the hot cream mixture into the yolk mixture, then gradually whisk the yolk mixture into the hot cream. Cook over medium heat, stirring constantly, until the custard thickens. To check for doneness, draw your finger through the custard on the back of the spoon; it should leave a trail.

Pour the hot custard over the chocolate and whisk until the chocolate is melted and the mixture is blended. Strain the custard through

a fine-mesh sieve, cover, and refrigerate until completely chilled, at least 6 hours.

Preheat the oven to 350°F. Butter six 4-ounce porcelain ramekins or pot-de-crème pots. Prepare a water bath by placing a terry-cloth washcloth in the bottom of a roasting or similar-style pan, and arrange the ramekins on top of it. (This prevents the ramekins from sliding, insulates their bottoms, and helps prevent overcooking.)

Scoop the chilled custard into the ramekins. Fill the roasting pan with enough hot water to reach halfway up the sides of the ramekins. Bake, covered, until the outsides are set and the middles still jiggle, about 25 minutes. Remove the ramekins from the water bath and transfer to a wire rack to cool to room temperature. Refrigerate, covered, until 30 minutes before serving.

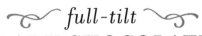

full-tilt
DARK CHOCOLATE
with ZABAGLIONE

Serves
6

HERE'S AN ELEGANT NEW SLANT ON AN OLD-FASHIONED
dessert ingredient: gelatin. I know what you're thinking: chocolate and gelatin?
Believe me, not only does the combination work, but you'll get lots of compli-
ments on this dessert's unusual presentation. People won't be able to figure out
how you got the chocolate gelée and zabaglione to slant at such an interesting
angle. That won't keep them from dipping their spoons into the classic Italian
custard, along with the brilliant chocolate. One taste and it's full-tilt ahead.

CHOCOLATE
2½ teaspoons (1 package) unflavored
   gelatin
1½ cups tepid water, divided
½ cup heavy (whipping) cream
⅓ cup firmly packed dark brown sugar
¼ cup premium unsweetened Dutch-
   process cocoa powder

ZABAGLIONE
5 large egg yolks, at room
   temperature
5 teaspoons granulated sugar
⅓ cup sweet Marsala
1 cup heavy (whipping) cream,
   whipped and chilled

TO MAKE THE SLANT: You will need to find a prop to set 6 narrow,
6-ounce dessert glasses at an angle. (I used small paperback books.)
Take 1 glass and fill it with ⅓ cup water. On a baking tray, prop the
glass at an angle so that the water comes ¼ to ½ inch from its rim and
support the glass at that angle. Then, use small pieces of floral putty
(or other nonpermanent putty) to prop the rest of the glasses at the
same angle. Empty the water from the first glass and prop it with floral
putty as well. Set aside.

continued

TO MAKE THE CHOCOLATE: In a small saucepan, sprinkle the gelatin over ½ cup of the water and let stand for 1 minute to soften. Cook over low heat, stirring, until the gelatin dissolves, 1 to 2 minutes. Remove from the heat.

Meanwhile, in a heavy, 1-quart saucepan, gently whisk the remaining 1 cup water, the cream, brown sugar, and cocoa powder until blended and bring just to a boil. Remove from the heat and stir in the gelatin mixture until combined. Let the mixture cool slightly, then divide the chocolate among the prepared glasses, about ⅓ cup each. You may find a funnel helps to control the chocolate as you pour it into the glasses. (Any leftovers can be poured into a small dish for the cook to sample.) Carefully transfer the pan with the glasses to the refrigerator, and refrigerate until firm.

TO MAKE THE ZABAGLIONE: It doesn't take long, and the fresher the better. About 15 minutes before serving, in a double boiler, combine the egg yolks with the sugar. Using a whisk or hand mixer with a whisk attachment, whip the mixture until pale, about 3 minutes. Place over barely simmering water and add the Marsala, whisking continuously until the mixture is thick, foamy, and warm to the touch, about 4 minutes. Remove from the heat and continue whisking until the zabaglione has cooled slightly.

Fold the slightly cooled zabaglione into the whipped cream. Remove the chilled chocolate from the refrigerator and, holding each glass at a 45-degree angle, slowly fill the empty space with zabaglione, gradually righting the glass as you fill it. Repeat with remaining glasses and serve immediately.

black and white SOUFFLÉ

serves 4

JANE ZWINGER, MY FRIEND AND FELLOW CHOCOLATE
lover, adds an element of surprise to her version of a chocolate soufflé. She pairs
a bittersweet chocolate layer with one of sweet white chocolate. The contrast
and the taste are outstanding.

2 tablespoons granulated sugar,
  divided

1⅓ cups milk, plus more as needed

6 large sprigs fresh mint

3 ounces premium white chocolate
  such as Green & Black's, Valrhona,
  Callebaut, or El Rey, finely chopped

2 ounces premium dark chocolate
  (70%), finely chopped

1 tablespoon premium unsweetened
  Dutch-process cocoa powder

2 tablespoons unsalted butter, plus
  more for the dish

3 tablespoons all-purpose flour

4 large eggs, separated, at room
  temperature

1 large egg white, at room
  temperature

5 tablespoons superfine sugar
  (see Note, page 122)

Powdered sugar for dusting

Preheat the oven to 350°F. Generously butter the inside of a 1½-quart
soufflé dish, then coat with 1 tablespoon granulated sugar, including
the rim. Chill until ready to use.

In a small saucepan over medium-high heat, heat the 1½ cups milk
and the mint sprigs until small bubbles form around the edges of the
pan. Remove from the heat, cover, and steep for 30 minutes. Remove
the sprigs and squeeze out the excess milk. Strain into a 2-cup measuring cup, adding additional milk as needed to make 1¼ cups total.

continued

Put the white chocolate in a medium bowl. Put the dark chocolate and cocoa in another medium bowl. In a small, heavy saucepan over low heat, melt the 2 tablespoons butter. Blend in the flour and cook, stirring, for 3 to 5 minutes (cooking this long minimizes the "flour" taste). You do not want the flour to brown. Slowly add the mint-infused milk, stirring constantly, until smooth and thickened. Remove from the heat and measure ½ cup plus 2 tablespoons sauce. Pour it over the white chocolate. Pour the remaining ½ cup plus 2 tablespoons sauce over the dark chocolate. Let both mixtures stand for several minutes, then stir until the chocolates are melted and the mixtures are smooth. Cool to lukewarm. Whisk 2 egg yolks into each bowl of chocolate until blended.

In a stand mixer with the whisk attachment, whisk the egg white until foamy. Gradually add the superfine sugar and whisk until stiff peaks form. Do not overbeat. Scoop out half the egg white and gently fold them into the white chocolate until just incorporated. Repeat with the remaining egg white and the dark chocolate. Scoop out ¼ cup of the dark chocolate mixture and set aside. Spoon the remainder into the bottom of the prepared dish. Then, spoon and gently spread the white chocolate mixture on top. Center the scoop of reserved dark chocolate on top (as the soufflé bakes, the dark chocolate will be incorporated into the top as a design).

Bake the soufflé until fragrant and fully risen, about 25 minutes. The exterior will resemble the top of a sponge cake. Dust the soufflé with powdered sugar. Present it in the souffle dish and serve immediately by spooning into individual bowls.

NOTE

Superfine sugar, also called baker's sugar, is available in supermarket baking sections. For a quick substitute, whirl 1 cup of granulated sugar at a time in a food processor or blender until fine, about 30 seconds.

CHILLED CHOCOLATE DESSERTS
and
ICE CREAMS

devil's halos with fire-and-brimstone fudge sauce
126

Bittersweet Chocolate-Rum Icebox Cake
129

Mom's Frozen Fudge Pops
131

ARTISAN CHOCOLATE SORBET
132

Deep, Dark Chocolate Ice Cream
134

devil's halos with
FIRE-AND-BRIMSTONE
FUDGE SAUCE

makes
6
SERVINGS

THE NAME OF THIS SINFUL YET DIVINE DESSERT REFERS TO the devilishly good halo-shaped meringues and the little rivers of chile-laced fudge sauce that stream down the ice cream onto the meringues and the plate. Every spoonful—a little heat and a little cold—is pure delight. If you prefer, substitute our chocolate ice cream (page 134) for the vanilla.

MERINGUE HALOS
¾ cup granulated sugar

2 tablespoons premium unsweetened cocoa powder

1½ teaspoons instant coffee powder

3 large egg whites, at room temperature or slightly warm

⅜ teaspoon cream of tartar

SAUCE
1½ cups heavy (whipping) cream

3 tablespoons plus 1 teaspoon chopped dried chipotle chiles

4 ounces premium dark chocolate, chopped

1 quart premium vanilla-bean ice cream, homemade or purchased

Premium cacao nibs, ground Cacao-Nib Crunch (page 174); or finely ground espresso for garnish

Ground chile powder for garnish

TO MAKE THE HALOS: Preheat the oven to 200°F. Line a baking sheet with parchment paper. Draw six 3½-inch circles on the parchment, leaving at least 1 inch between circles. Turn the parchment over, pencil side down.

In a small bowl, whisk the sugar, cocoa, and coffee powder until blended. In the bowl of a stand mixer fitted with the whisk attachment, whisk the egg whites and cream of tartar on medium-low speed, until foamy. Increase the speed to medium-high, and gradually add the sugar mixture, whisking until stiff, not dry, peaks form, about 2½ minutes. Increase the speed to high and continue to whisk until stiff and glossy, about 4 minutes.

For each halo, use a teaspoon to drop a 1-inch dollop of meringue onto the edge of a circle on the parchment. Drop a second spoonful next to the first so that they connect. Repeat to form a circle, using about 10 dollops per circle. Repeat until all the circles are completed, using any leftover meringue to make individual kisses. Bake for 3 hours, or until dry throughout. Test by checking one of the individual kisses. If the halos need to dry further, turn off the oven and leave them inside, with the door shut, for 30 to 90 minutes. Transfer the halos on the parchment paper to wire racks to cool completely. Carefully peel the halos off the parchment when cooled. Use now or store in an airtight container for up to 2 weeks.

TO MAKE THE SAUCE: In a small saucepan over medium-high heat, combine the cream and dried chipotles and heat until small bubbles appear around the edges of the pan. Remove from the heat, cover, and steep for 30 minutes. Using a fine-mesh sieve, strain out the chiles, pressing them to release any liquid. Discard the chiles. Rinse out the saucepan and return the cream to it. Reheat until small bubbles appear around the edges of the pan. Put the chocolate in a small bowl and pour the hot milk over it. Let stand for 3 minutes, then stir until smooth. Transfer to a small pitcher for easy pouring.

TO ASSEMBLE THE HALOS: Arrange each meringue on a dessert plate. Place a scoop of ice cream in the center of each. Drizzle the warm sauce over the ice cream, letting it trickle over the meringue onto the plate. Sprinkle each dessert as well as the plate with a grinding of cacao nibs and a pinch of chile powder. In addition, if desired, pass the pepper grinder containing the nibs at the table.

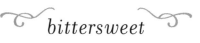

bittersweet CHOCOLATE-RUM ICEBOX CAKE

Serves 16

HERE'S A STUNNING ICEBOX CAKE THAT'S UNDERSTATED simplicity at its best. Great for entertaining, it serves 16 and can be made in advance. In this soufflé-dish version, rum-dipped ladyfingers surround a rich, bittersweet-chocolate mousse, with an extra layer of cookies running through the middle. After the cake is made and chilled (no baking involved), it's inverted onto a cake plate, ready for your finishing touches. A dusting of powdered sugar? A sprinkling of cocoa powder? If not, chocolate curls or a satiny ribbon of dark chocolate sauce also make an elegant statement.

¾ cup granulated sugar, divided

¾ cup plus 2 tablespoons water

¾ cup light rum

About 32 ladyfingers (two 7-ounce packages)

5 ounces premium dark chocolate, chopped

½ cup powdered sugar

2 large eggs, separated and divided

½ cup (1 stick) unsalted butter, at room temperature, plus more for the dish

1 large egg white

Unsweetened cocoa powder and powdered sugar for dusting

Chocloate Curls for garnish (page 110)

Butter a 2-quart soufflé dish. Cut a circle of parchment to fit the bottom and press into place. Cut a strip of parchment the same width as the height of the soufflé dish. Fit it around the sides and press into place.

In a small saucepan over medium-high heat, combine ½ cup of the sugar and ¾ cup of the water and boil for 2 minutes. Remove from the heat and stir in the rum. Let cool slightly. Dip (do not soak) enough

continued

ladyfingers in the sugar syrup, one at a time, to stand, side-by-side, around the inside of the soufflé dish. To line the bottom of the dish (which will be the top of the cake once it is unmolded), dip and coat 4 to 5 ladyfingers in the syrup, cutting their ends at an angle to make them fit. (Remember, they form the cake's top so you will want an attractive placement.) Reserve the remaining rum mixture.

Place the chocolate and the remaining 2 tablespoons water in a medium heatproof bowl and set in a wide pan or skillet of hot water. Set aside for 5 minutes, stirring 4 or 5 times, and let it melt completely. Stir until smooth. Gradually stir in the powdered sugar. Add the 2 egg yolks, one at a time, beating well after each addition. Add the ½ cup butter, 2 to 3 tablespoons at a time, stirring until each addition is melted. When all is combined, remove from the heat and let cool for 20 minutes.

In a stand mixer fitted with the whisk attachment, whisk the 3 egg whites until foamy. Increase the speed to medium-high and gradually add the remaining ¼ cup sugar. Increase the speed to high and beat until stiff, but not dry, peaks form. Do not overbeat. Gently fold one-quarter of the beaten egg whites into the chocolate mixture to lighten it. Fold in the remaining egg whites until just incorporated and no large streaks of egg white remain.

Spread half the chocolate mixture into the prepared dish. Dip and coat 4 to 5 more ladyfingers in the syrup and cut to fit, creating a middle layer. Spread the remaining chocolate mixture over the lady-fingers. Dip and coat the final 4 to 5 ladyfingers to cover the top and gently press into place. Cover and refrigerate overnight.

To serve, invert the dish onto a serving plate. The cake will slip out of its lining. Carefully peel the parchment paper off the bottom of the cake. To garnish, dust the top of the cake with powdered sugar, cocoa, or a combination of both. For added panache, cap the top with a crown or garland of chocolate curls.

mom's
FROZEN
FUDGE POPS

makes
6
FROZEN POPS

EVERY SUMMER MY MOM MADE THESE OUT-OF-THIS-WORLD
fudgy frozen pops for my brother and me. The recipe is almost identical to that
for Mom's Real Chocolate Pudding (page 109), except here she uses cocoa
powder instead of chocolate, and rich whole milk instead of the evaporated kind.

3 cups 3.5% milk or a combination of
   whole milk and half-and-half,
   divided

¾ cup granulated sugar

¼ teaspoon salt

¾ cup premium unsweetened cocoa
   powder

1½ teaspoons cornstarch

First, have patience, and don't try to hurry the process. In the top of a
double boiler, combine 2 cups of the milk, the sugar, and salt and place
over simmering water. Cook, stirring occasionally, until the milk is hot.

Meanwhile, in a medium bowl, whisk the remaining 1 cup milk, the
cocoa, and cornstarch until thick and combined. Let rest until the milk
is hot, then scrape the mixture into the double boiler and cook, stirring
occasionally to begin with and more frequently toward the end, 12 to
17 minutes. The mixture will turn a thick, rich brown.

Remove from the heat and cool, stirring occasionally. When the mixture
is lukewarm, cover the surface with plastic wrap so a skin does not form.

When the mixture is at room temperature, pour into six 4-ounce pop
molds, leaving about ½ inch of space at the top (as the pops freeze, they
will expand). Insert the handles and freeze for 4 hours or more. Remove
each pop from its mold by gently squeezing the pop as you pull the handle.
If it won't slide out, run the mold under warm water a few seconds.

artisan
CHOCOLATE
SORBET

makes about

3

CUPS
SORBET

TO MAKE THIS REFRESHING, BRIGHT-TASTING SORBET, use a premium chocolate, one whose flavor and complexity you enjoy as an eating chocolate. (Once, a craving left me no choice but to use a supermarket staple. The unpleasant aftertaste was a lesson.) This sorbet is an excellent partner for many of the desserts in this book, including the One-Bite-to-Heaven Chocolate Yeast Cake (page 72) and Wednesday Wild's Wintertime Chocolate-Caramel Tart (page 100).

8 ounces premium dark chocolate (no higher than 62%), chopped
¼ cup granulated sugar
1²/₃ cups just-off-the-boil water

¼ cup Lazzaroni Amaretto or other premium almond liqueur (optional)
Candied violets or rose petals for garnish (optional)

Place the chocolate and sugar in a medium bowl. Pour the water over the chocolate and stir until the chocolate is melted and the mixture is blended (there may be pinhole-sized chocolate spots along the sides of the bowl). If desired, stir in the liqueur until blended. Cool completely, stirring occasionally.

Refrigerate for 2 to 3 hours, stirring from time to time. For a smooth finish, do not chill longer. Stir the mixture to blend, then pour it into an ice-cream maker. Freeze according to the manufacturer's instructions. Place the sorbet in a 1-quart container, cover, and freeze for 4 to 6 hours or overnight. To make serving easier, dip your scoop in warm water before using it. If desired, garnish servings with candied violets or rose petals.

deep, dark
CHOCOLATE
ICE CREAM

makes about

3
CUPS
ICE CREAM

THIS IS A SERIOUS CHOCOLATE ICE CREAM. IT HAS A gloss and chill that yield to the warmth of your palate and a taste that is luscious and deep. From the first bite, you'll detect the fine chocolate. The extra step of caramelizing the sugar is what sets this ice cream apart.

The key to making great ice cream is in the ingredients, not in the ice-cream maker. Work with superior chocolate and cocoa powder and you'll reap the rewards. I use an automatic Cuisinart ICE-25 ice-cream maker ($40 to $60 online). As long as I put in delicious ingredients, it turns out delicious ice cream.

2 cups whole milk or half-and-half, divided

¾ cup granulated sugar, divided

3½ ounces premium dark chocolate (no higher than 62%), chopped

½ cup premium unsweetened cocoa powder

2 tablespoons premium unsweetened Dutch-process cocoa powder

2 tablespoons water

5 large egg yolks, at room temperature

In the top of a double boiler, combine 1½ cups of the milk, ½ cup of the sugar, the chocolate, and the unsweetened and Dutch-process cocoas. Place over simmering water and cook, stirring occasionally, until the chocolate melts and the mixture is hot and blended. Keep warm over low heat.

Meanwhile, in a small, heavy saucepan with a pale interior, combine the remaining ¼ cup of sugar with the water. Over medium heat, stir until the sugar dissolves, then let it cook until the mixture turns amber. Remove from the heat and slowly add the remaining ½ cup of milk. The mixture will foam. Return to the heat and stir until the sugar dissolves, then stir into the chocolate mixture.

In a small bowl, whisk the egg yolks briefly. Gradually whisk ½ cup of the hot chocolate mixture into the yolk mixture, then gradually whisk the yolk mixture into the hot chocolate mixture. Cook over simmering water, stirring, until the custard thickens, 5 to 7 minutes. To check for doneness, draw your finger through the custard on the back of the spoon; it should leave a trail. Remove from the heat, and continue to stir the custard for a few minutes so that it doesn't overcook.

Strain the custard through a fine-mesh sieve and cool completely. Cover and refrigerate for at least 3 hours or up to 3 days. Stir the mixture to blend, then pour it into an ice-cream maker. Freeze according to the manufacturer's instructions. After the ice cream is made, let it cure in the freezer at least 3 hours before serving. To make serving easier, dip your scoop in warm water before using it.

FUDGY SAUCES *and* CHOCOLATE FONDUES

old-fashioned
HOT FUDGE
SAUCE

makes about
1 ¼
CUPS
SAUCE

FIVE YEARS AGO, THIS TRADITIONAL HOT FUDGE SAUCE
would have required half as much chocolate and twice as much sugar, but
tastes have changed. Today, the real flavor of chocolate is what we crave. Here
is an updated version I use for hot fudge sundaes and full-fledged banana splits.
When the warm, satiny chocolate flows over ice cream, the sauce becomes
slightly chewy and reminiscent of soda-fountain extravaganzas crowned with
billowing whipped cream and bright, red cherries.

4 ounces premium unsweetened
  chocolate, chopped
2 tablespoons unsalted butter, cut into
  pieces, at room temperature
½ cup boiling water
½ cup granulated sugar

3 tablespoons dark or light corn
  syrup
¼ teaspoon salt
½ teaspoon pure vanilla extract
  (optional)

Place the chocolate and butter in a small saucepan and set in a wide
pan or skillet of hot water. Set aside for 5 minutes, stirring 4 or 5 times,
and let the chocolate melt completely. Stir until smooth, then add the
boiling water, sugar, and corn syrup and mix until blended. Place the
saucepan over medium-high heat and bring the sauce to a gentle boil.
Once it begins to bubble, do not stir. For a thick sauce that becomes
slightly chewy over ice cream, gently boil, covered, for 3 minutes. (For
an even thicker sauce, gently boil, uncovered, for an additional 3 minutes.) Remove from the heat, let cool slightly, and stir in the salt.

After the sauce is cool enough to taste, try it, then add the vanilla, if desired. If you make the sauce ahead, rewarm it briefly in a pan of hot water or in a microwave for 1 to 1½ minutes, stirring several times, until the sauce is shiny and smooth. Any unused portion can be kept in a closed container in the refrigerator for a week or frozen up to 3 months.

VARIATION

For **As-You-Like-It Hot Fudge Sauce**, follow the main recipe, substituting your favorite liqueur or spirit, such as Grand Marnier, Kahlúa, or premium bourbon, for the optional ¼ teaspoon vanilla. For best results, begin with 1 tablespoon liqueur, then adjust the flavoring by adding more, according to taste.

jane's one-and-only
BITTERSWEET CHOCOLATE
SAUCE

makes about

2 1/2

CUPS
SAUCE

THIS CHOCOLATE SAUCE IS THE TIME-HONORED FAVORITE
of my friend and fellow cook Jane Zwinger. You can see how easy it is to make.
No wonder this is the recipe Jane turns to when she wants a voluptuous,
bittersweet chocolate sauce to top vanilla-bean ice cream.

No cream? Don't worry. Replacing the cream with milk or half-and-half
will only intensify the taste of the chocolate (another reason to use the best
chocolate you can buy). While the feel of the sauce will not be as rich in the
mouth (because there is less fat), it will still be marvelous.

¾ cup heavy (whipping) cream
⅓ cup granulated sugar
4 tablespoons unsalted butter, cut into
pieces

¼ cup water
10 ounces premium dark chocolate,
chopped

In a medium saucepan over medium-high heat, combine the cream,
sugar, butter, and water and bring to a gentle boil. Remove from the
heat, add the chocolate, cover, and wait 5 minutes. Gently whisk into a
smooth, creamy sauce. The warm sauce is ready to use. If made ahead,
rewarm briefly in a pan of hot water or in a microwave on low power
for 1 to 1½ minutes, stirring several times, until the sauce is shiny and
smooth. Any leftover sauce can be kept in an airtight container in the
refrigerator for a week or frozen up to 3 months.

fast and fantastic
ARTISAN
CHOCOLATE SAUCE
makes a little less than
1
CUP
SAUCE

DO CACAO PERCENTAGES AND EXPENSIVE SINGLE-ORIGIN estate chocolates (see page 19) leave you feeling confused, though you'd love to make something simple using a spectacular artisan chocolate bar? If so, this smooth, rich, silky, and effortless topping is the one for you. It's a good example of how the simplest recipe—a two-ingredient sauce—can be the ideal way to show off a complex and interesting chocolate.

For this recipe, I often use a bar of Dagoba's Chocolate Infusions, such as their Mint (59%) (mint/rosemary), Roseberry (59%) (rosemary/rose hips), or Xocolati (74%) (chiles/nibs).

2 ounces premium artisan dark chocolate bar, chopped	½ cup plus 2 tablespoons heavy (whipping) cream

Place the chocolate and cream in a medium, heatproof bowl in a pan or wide skillet of hot water. Set aside for 5 minutes, then stir and allow the mixture to melt completely. Stir until smooth. The warm sauce is ready to serve.

If made ahead, rewarm briefly in a pan of hot water or in a microwave on low power for 1 to 1½ minutes, stirring several times, until the sauce is shiny and smooth. Any leftover sauce can be kept in an airtight container in the refrigerator for a week or frozen up to 3 months.

brown sugar
COCOA
SAUCE

makes about
2
CUPS
SAUCE

A RICH, FUDGY SAUCE WITH HINTS OF CARAMEL, THIS
cocoa-based sauce packs a lot of flavor. It uses five simple ingredients and
goes together with a stir. The perfect last-minute sauce for a first-rate sundae,
or any ice cream you happen to find in the freezer.

1 cup firmly packed dark brown sugar

1 cup heavy (whipping) cream

¼ cup premium unsweetened cocoa
powder

2 tablespoons unsalted butter

Pinch of salt

In a medium saucepan over medium-low heat, combine the brown
sugar, cream, cocoa, butter, and salt. Bring to a boil, stirring or gently
whisking until the butter has melted and the mixture is blended and
smooth. Remove from the heat and cool for 30 to 40 minutes to allow
the sauce to thicken and develop its flavor. Gently stir before serving.

If made ahead, rewarm briefly in a pan of hot water or in a microwave on low power for 1 to 1½ minutes, stirring several times, until the
sauce is shiny and smooth. Any unused portion can be kept in an airtight container in the refrigerator for a week or frozen up to 3 months.

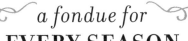

a fondue for EVERY SEASON

Serves 4 to 6
EACH RECIPE YIELDS
ABOUT 1⅓ CUPS

I LOVE THIS QUARTET OF UPDATED CLASSIC CHOCOLATE fondues. They're such good, simple desserts because they're easy to make and fun to experiment with. I like to serve these fondues in individual portions, with everyone getting their own small bowl accompanied with a sampling of "dippers," but you also can serve them family-style. Since the dippers are eminently adaptable to what might be in season (or in the cookie jar or pantry), I've given suggestions. You can take it from there.

WINTER FONDUE

1 cup heavy (whipping) cream

2 to 3 tablespoons whole juniper berries, crushed

12 ounces premium dark chocolate, chopped

SUGGESTED DIPPERS
(choose at least 3):

Fresh apples, bananas, or other regional fresh fruit, sliced or cut up for dipping

Seedless grape clusters

Orange, grapefruit, tangerine, or blood orange segments

Caramel Crackers (page 179) or nut brittle, broken into pieces for dipping

Large, fresh marshmallows

One-Bite-to-Heaven Chocolate Yeast Cake (page 72), cut into cubes

Homemade or purchased pound cake, cut into cubes

Biscotti, shortbread, or meringue-kiss cookies, available at international groceries such as Trader Joe's

Fresh baguette, sliced

Additional small dipping bowls of cacao nibs, sea salt, pepper blends, and olive oil

A sprinkling of fresh pomegranate seeds for garnish

continued

In a small saucepan over medium-high heat, combine the cream and juniper berries and heat until small bubbles appear around the edges of the pan. Remove from the heat, cover, and steep for 30 minutes. Using a fine-mesh sieve, strain out the juniper berries, pressing to release any liquid. Discard the juniper berries.

Place the chocolate in a medium bowl. Reheat the infused cream until simmering. Pour the cream over the chocolate. Let stand for 2 to 3 minutes, then gently whisk until the mixture is very smooth. To keep warm until serving time, set the bowl in a shallow pan of hot water. Serve warm in individual portions or family-style with a selection of dippers.

SPRING FONDUE

1 cup heavy (whipping) cream

2 Earl Grey tea bags

12 ounces premium dark chocolate, chopped

Grated zest from 1 small organic orange

SUGGESTED DIPPERS
(choose at least 3):

Caramel Crackers (page 179) or nut brittle, broken into pieces for dipping

One-Bite-to-Heaven Chocolate Yeast Cake (page 72), cut into cubes

Homemade or purchased pound cake, cut into cubes

Biscotti, shortbread, or meringue-kiss cookies, available at international groceries such as Trader Joe's

Fresh baguette, sliced

Additional small dipping bowls of cacao nibs, sea salt, pepper blends, and olive oil

In a small saucepan over medium-high heat, combine the cream and tea bags and heat until small bubbles appear around the edges of the pan. Remove from the heat, cover, and steep for 30 minutes. Remove the tea bags, pressing them to release any liquid. Discard the tea bags.

Place the chocolate in a medium bowl. Reheat the infused cream until simmering. Pour the cream over the chocolate. Let stand for 2 to 3 minutes, then gently whisk until the mixture is very smooth. To keep warm until serving time, set the bowl in a shallow pan of hot water. Serve warm, sprinkled with orange zest, in individual portions or family-style with a selection of dippers.

SUMMER FONDUE

1 cup heavy (whipping) cream

2 teaspoons dried culinary lavender

12 ounces premium dark chocolate, chopped

SUGGESTED DIPPERS
(choose at least 3):

Fresh berries, figs, cherries, or other regional fresh fruit, sliced or cut up for dipping

Caramel Crackers (page 179) or nut brittle, broken into pieces for dipping

Large, fresh marshmallows

Large fresh mint leaves

One-Bite-to-Heaven Chocolate Yeast Cake (page 72), cut into cubes

Homemade or purchased pound cake, cut into cubes

Biscotti, shortbread, or meringue-kiss cookies, available at international groceries such as Trader Joe's

Additional small dipping bowls of cacao nibs, sea salt, pepper blends, and olive oil

In a small saucepan over medium-high heat, combine the cream and lavender and heat until small bubbles appear around the edges of the pan. Remove from the heat, cover, and steep for 30 minutes. Using a fine-mesh sieve, strain out the lavender, pressing to release any liquid. Discard the lavender.

Place the chocolate in a medium bowl. Reheat the infused cream until simmering. Pour the cream over the chocolate. Let stand for 2 to 3 minutes, then gently whisk until the mixture is very smooth. To keep warm until serving time, set the bowl in a shallow pan of hot water. Serve warm in individual portions or family-style with a selection of dippers.

continued

FALL FONDUE

1 cup heavy (whipping) cream

One 4-inch cinnamon stick, crushed with a meat tenderizer

1½ teaspoons peeled and chopped fresh ginger

½ teaspoon whole cloves, crushed with a meat tenderizer

12 ounces premium dark chocolate, chopped

SUGGESTED DIPPERS
(choose at least 3):

Fresh pears, apples, pineapples, or other regional fresh fruit, sliced or cut up for dipping

Dried figs, prunes, and other dried fruit slices such as apricot, pear, mango, papaya, or pineapple

Whole toasted almonds or other large nuts

Caramel Crackers (page 179) or nut brittle, broken into pieces for dipping

One-Bite-to-Heaven Chocolate Yeast Cake (page 72), cut into cubes

Homemade or purchased pound cake, cut into cubes

Biscotti, shortbread, or meringue-kiss cookies, available at international groceries such as Trader Joe's

Fresh baguette, sliced

Additional small dipping bowls of cacao nibs, sea salt, pepper blends, and olive oil

In a small saucepan over medium-high heat, combine the cream, cinnamon, ginger, and cloves and heat until small bubbles appear around the edges of the pan. Remove from the heat, cover, and steep for 30 minutes. Using a fine-mesh sieve, strain out the spices, pressing to release any liquid. Discard the spices.

Place the chocolate in a medium bowl. Reheat the infused cream until simmering. Pour the cream over the chocolate. Let stand for 2 to 3 minutes, then gently whisk until the mixture is very smooth. To keep warm until serving time, set the bowl in a shallow pan of hot water. Serve warm in individual portions or family-style with a selection of dippers.

BREAKFAST DELIGHTS
and
SMALL BITES

THE PERRY FAMILY'S FAVORITE CHOCOLATE STICKY BUNS
150

"You Made These?" Chocolate Morning Biscuits

152

chocolate dream scones with mascarpone spread
154

Hot Chocolate Waffles with Chocolate-Hazelnut Spread
157

BITTERSWEET CHOCOLATE-CARAMEL APPLE SLICES
159

cool-hand chocolate pretzels
162

the perry family's
FAVORITE
CHOCOLATE STICKY BUNS

makes
12
STICKY BUNS

THESE TRADITIONAL STICKY BUNS WITH THEIR DARK COCOA- caramel-pecan topping are sure to become one of your signature recipes. I adapted the recipe from an old *Pepperidge Farm* cookbook more than thirty years ago and my family tells me we couldn't have a birthday breakfast without them. While everyone loves the topping, I think the best part is the cinnamon-and-sugar filling dotted with dark chocolate that swirls, jelly-roll style, through each bun.

BUNS
2 to 2¼ teaspoons (1 package) active dry yeast
⅓ cup warm (110° to 115°F) water
¾ cup milk
½ cup (1 stick) unsalted butter, at room temperature
⅓ cup granulated sugar
1 teaspoon salt
3½ to 4 cups all-purpose or bread flour, divided
1 large egg, at room temperature

TOPPING
½ cup (1 stick) unsalted butter, plus more for the pan

1 cup firmly packed light brown sugar
¼ cup light corn syrup
3 tablespoons premium unsweetened cocoa powder
½ cup chopped pecans or walnuts

FILLING
⅔ cup granulated sugar
4 teaspoons premium unsweetened cocoa powder
1½ teaspoons ground cinnamon
2 tablespoons unsalted butter, melted
2½ ounces premium dark chocolate, chopped

TO MAKE THE BUNS: In a small bowl, sprinkle the yeast over the warm water and stir to combine. In a small saucepan over medium heat, warm the milk and add the butter, sugar, and salt, stirring until the butter melts. Transfer to the large bowl of a stand mixer and let cool to lukewarm.

Add ¾ cup of the flour to the milk mixture and mix on low speed until blended, about 1 minute. Add the egg and beat on medium speed until well combined, scraping down the sides and bottom of the bowl as necessary. Beat in the yeast mixture until well blended. Gradually stir in enough of the remaining flour, a little at a time, to make a soft dough that pulls away from the sides of the bowl.

Using the dough hook on your mixer (or turning it out onto a lightly floured work surface), knead until smooth, satiny, and no longer sticky, 5 to 8 minutes. Transfer the dough to a lightly greased, large bowl and rotate the dough to grease the top. Cover the bowl with plastic wrap and let the dough rise in a warm place until doubled in size, about 1 hour. Once the dough has doubled, press down, replace the plastic wrap, and let it rest for 10 minutes.

TO MAKE THE TOPPING: Lightly grease a 9-by-13-inch metal baking pan with butter or cooking spray. In a saucepan over medium heat, melt the ½ cup butter. Stir in the brown sugar, corn syrup, and cocoa powder. Bring to a boil and cook for 1 minute. Pour the syrup into the prepared pan and tilt the pan so the topping evenly coats the bottom. Sprinkle the pecans over the brown-sugar sauce.

TO MAKE THE FILLING: In a small bowl, mix the sugar, cocoa, and cinnamon until blended. Using a rolling pin, shape the dough into a 12-by-8-inch rectangle, with a long side toward you. Brush the dough with the melted butter. Sprinkle the filling over the buttered dough, leaving a ½-inch border at the far edge. Sprinkle the buttered filling with the chopped chocolate. Roll up the dough lengthwise, beginning with the long edge closest to you. Moisten the border with water and pinch the ends to form secure seams. Cut the roll into 12 slices and place each slice, cut side down, into the prepared pan. Cover with plastic wrap and let rise in a warm, draft-free spot until doubled, about 40 minutes.

Preheat the oven to 350°F. Bake until the buns are golden, about 27 minutes. Turn out of the pan immediately onto a large serving platter. Let cool for about 5 minutes before serving. The buns are best eaten warm or at room temperature within hours of baking.

"you made these?" CHOCOLATE MORNING BISCUITS

makes
12
BISCUITS

THIS RECIPE IS QUICK, EASY, AND PERFECT FOR MORNINGS
when you're craving good chocolate as well as extra attention. ("You made these?" "They're *fabulous!*") The rich spiral swirl of dark, melting chocolate gives these warm-from-the-oven biscuits an elegant, pastrylike flavor.

DOUGH
2 cups all-purpose flour

1 tablespoon granulated sugar

1 tablespoon baking powder

½ teaspoon salt

5 tablespoons cold unsalted butter, cut into small pieces

¾ cup whole milk

FILLING
3 tablespoons unsalted butter, softened

2 tablespoons granulated sugar

1 bar (3½ to 4 ounces) premium dark chocolate, finely chopped, but leaving some ¼-inch chunks

TOPPING (OPTIONAL)
1 large egg yolk

1 tablespoon whole milk

Granulated sugar for sprinkling

TO MAKE THE DOUGH: Preheat the oven to 400°F. Line a baking sheet with parchment paper. In a medium bowl, whisk the flour, sugar, baking powder, and salt until well blended.

Using your fingers or a pastry blender, work the butter into the dry ingredients until crumbly and some pea-sized pieces of butter remain. Add the milk and stir with a fork, until a rough dough forms.

Turn out the dough onto a lightly floured work surface. Using lightly floured hands, gently form a ball, then gently knead the dough 8 to 10 times. Using a floured rolling pin, roll into a 13-by-11-inch rectangle, arranging the long side near you.

TO ADD THE FILLING: Spread the butter on the dough, then sprinkle with the sugar and the chocolate. Beginning with one long side, snugly roll up the dough in jelly-roll fashion. Using a sharp knife, cut the roll crosswise into 12 slices. Arrange the slices, cut side down, 2 inches apart on the prepared baking sheet.

TO ADD THE TOPPING (IF DESIRED): In a cup, mix the egg yolk and milk until blended. Brush the biscuit tops with the egg wash and sprinkle with sugar.

Bake the biscuits until golden and puffed, about 18 minutes. Transfer to a wire rack to cool for 5 minutes. The biscuits are best eaten warm or within several hours of baking.

chocolate DREAM SCONES
with MASCARPONE SPREAD

makes
16
SCONES AND ABOUT
2 CUPS SPREAD

IN EDINBURGH, AT THE LUXURIOUS BALMORAL HOTEL,
the chocolate lover's quintessential teatime treat must certainly be the Chocolate Dream Tea Service in the Bollinger Bar. It features an all-chocolate menu,
including chocolate scones with clotted cream and strawberry preserves. Without traveling so far, you can enjoy a flaky, dark—yet delicate—chocolate buttermilk
scone that will rival any others you've tasted. In case there's no clotted cream to
be found, the delicious mascarpone spread makes a perfect substitute.

SCONES
2 cups plus 2 tablespoons all-purpose
    flour
¼ cup plus 2 tablespoons unsweetened
    Dutch-process cocoa powder
⅓ cup granulated sugar
2½ teaspoons baking powder
½ teaspoon baking soda
½ teaspoon salt
¾ cup (1½ sticks) cold unsalted butter
1 cup buttermilk

SPREAD
1 tub (8 ounces) mascarpone cheese,
    at room temperature
½ cup heavy (whipping) cream
2 teaspoons granulated sugar
Scant ½ teaspoon pure vanilla extract

TO MAKE THE SCONES: Preheat the oven to 400°F. In a large bowl, whisk
the flour, cocoa, sugar, baking powder, baking soda, and salt until well
blended. Using the large holes of a flat grater, grate the cold butter into
the flour mixture and gently work with clean hands until it resembles
coarse crumbs.

continued

Make a well in the center of the flour-butter mixture and add the buttermilk all at once. Stir the mixture until the dough pulls away from the sides of the bowl. Using lightly floured hands, gather the dough into a soft ball and turn it out onto a lightly floured work surface. (Try and gather any loose bits, but don't worry if some dry particles remain.) Gently knead the dough 6 to 8 times on a lightly floured surface. Divide the dough into 4 parts and pat each one into a ¾-inch-thick circle. Cut each circle into 4 wedges.

Transfer the scones to an ungreased baking sheet. Bake until a tester inserted in the middle comes out as clean as it does toward the edge, 10 to 12 minutes. Serve warm with the mascarpone spread. The scones are best eaten within several hours of baking.

TO MAKE THE SPREAD: In a medium bowl, combine the mascarpone, cream, sugar, and vanilla until well combined and no lumps remain. Cover and refrigerate until well chilled. Remove 20 minutes before serving.

VARIATION

If you're nutty for chocolate scones and love hazelnuts, be sure to try **Hazelnut-Chocolate Scones with Chocolate-Hazelnut and Mascarpone Spreads**. Follow the main recipe, stirring ½ cup lightly toasted and chopped hazelnuts after the dough resembles coarse crumbs but before adding buttermilk. Proceed as directed and serve with a small bowl of chocolate-hazelnut spread (facing page)—or Nutella in a pinch—alongside the mascarpone spread.

hot chocolate WAFFLES WITH CHOCOLATE-HAZELNUT SPREAD

makes
12
4-INCH WAFFLES;
AND 1 CUP SPREAD

WE CALL THESE "DEADLINE WAFFLES" BECAUSE I MAKE them for my ten-year-old grandson Dylan when he's over at the house working on a book report for school. Somehow it makes the task easier. When I make the waffles for a weekend family breakfast, I serve them with chocolate-hazelnut spread, butter, and warm maple syrup. When Dylan is here alone, he often prefers a scoop of vanilla ice cream. It's a grandson's prerogative.

Feel free to alter the waffles by adding a few tablespoons of cacao nibs, ground cinnamon (about 1/4 teaspoon), and/or other earthy spices to the batter.

SPREAD

7 ounces premium dark chocolate, chopped

1/2 cup heavy (whipping) cream

1/4 cup ground hazelnuts

WAFFLES

2 ounces premium dark chocolate, chopped

6 tablespoons unsalted butter, cut into pieces

1 cup all-purpose flour

2 tablespoons premium unsweetened Dutch-process cocoa powder

2 teaspoons baking powder

1/4 teaspoon salt

3/4 cup buttermilk, at room temperature

1 large egg, at room temperature

1/2 teaspoon pure vanilla extract

1/4 cup granulated sugar

3 tablespoons firmly packed light or dark brown sugar

continued

TO MAKE THE SPREAD: Place the chocolate and cream in a medium heatproof bowl and set in a wide pan or skillet of hot water. Set aside for 5 minutes, stirring 4 or 5 times, and let the chocolate melt completely. Remove from the heat, stir in the hazelnuts, and let the mixture cool until it reaches a spreading consistency.

TO MAKE THE WAFFLES: Place the chocolate and butter in a medium heatproof bowl and set in a wide pan or skillet of hot water. Set aside for 5 minutes, stirring 4 or 5 times, and let melt completely. Stir occasionally until the mixture is smooth and cools slightly. In another medium bowl, whisk the flour, cocoa, baking powder, and salt until well blended.

In a medium bowl, whisk the buttermilk, egg, and vanilla until well blended. Whisk in the granulated and brown sugars. Add the dry ingredients and stir until just blended, scraping down the sides and bottom of the bowl as necessary.

Preheat the oven to 250°F. Heat a waffle iron and spray with cooking spray. Following the manufacturer's instructions, ladle the batter onto the waffle maker and cook until done. Keep the cooked waffles warm in the oven while you make more. Serve the waffles with chocolate-hazelnut spread or with butter and warm maple syrup.

NOTE

Did you know that waffles freeze well? Place any leftovers in a single layer on a baking sheet, freeze, then seal the waffles in a freezer-safe bag for up to 3 months. Warm in a toaster or in a 350°F oven for 10 minutes.

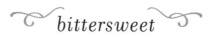

bittersweet
CHOCOLATE–CARAMEL
APPLE SLICES

serves
6 to 8

WHO CAN RESIST THIS DRESSED-UP VERSION OF A CARAMEL
apple, with its warm coating of caramel and chocolate? This simple yet elegant snack is one I often turn to when I need a quick dessert. There's always some caramel sauce in my refrigerator, so it's easy to assemble at the last minute. If I don't have apples, fresh pears or bananas will work just as well.

To serve a group, I arrange the apple slices on a narrow serving platter and set it in the middle of the table. For individual desserts, I place 4 to 6 apple slices on a small plate with 2 or 3 melon-ball-sized scoops of homemade ice cream such as Earl Grey Ice Cream (page 102).

CARAMEL SAUCE
1¼ cup granulated sugar

4 tablespoons unsalted butter, cut into pieces, at room temperature

¾ cup heavy (whipping) cream, at room temperature

½ teaspoon pure vanilla extract (optional)

¼ teaspoon salt

4 medium Granny Smith or Fuji apples, cored and cut into ½-inch slices

1 recipe Fast and Fantastic Artisan Chocolate Sauce (page 141), warmed

TO MAKE THE CARAMEL SAUCE: Before you begin, make sure you have everything next to the saucepan. Heat the sugar in a heavy 2- to 3-quart saucepan or Dutch oven with a pale interior over medium-high heat; use a whisk to occasionally stir the sugar as it begins to melt. As soon as

continued

the liquid sugar is a rich amber color, add the butter to the pan, whisking constantly until the butter melts. The mixture will foam slightly.

Immediately take the pan off the heat and slowly whisk in the cream. The mixture will foam again. Continue to whisk until the caramel is smooth. Let it cool about 15 minutes, stir in the vanilla and salt, then pour it into a 2-cup pitcher or measuring cup. If the sauce was made ahead, rewarm it briefly in a pan of hot water. Any unused portion can be kept in a closed container in the refrigerator for several days or frozen up to 3 months. Makes about 1¾ cups.

TO ASSEMBLE: On a serving platter, arrange the apple slices in one long line, all facing in the same direction. Pour a wide swath of warm caramel sauce down the row, followed by a smaller pour of the warmed chocolate sauce. Serve at once.

VARIATION

For a contemporary version of a classic, serve **Caramel and Chocolate Banana Splits with Earl Grey Ice Cream.** Follow the main recipe to create the caramel and chocolate sauces. For Earl Grey Ice Cream, see page 102. For each serving, substitute 1 small, peeled baby, Lady Finger, or Niño banana (about 3 inches long; available in many supermarkets), slicing it on the diagonal. Arrange the two halves, side by side, on a dessert plate. Add a Ping-Pong-ball-sized scoop of 1, 2, or 3 varieties of ice cream. Pour the caramel sauce down the center of each banana slice, then over the ice cream, followed by a long drizzle of chocolate sauce.

cool-hand CHOCOLATE PRETZELS

makes 2 to 3 DOZEN PRETZELS

WITH A TWIST AND A SWIRL, YOU CAN TURN AN ORDINARY
pretzel into the life of your next party. Paul Newman—Cool Hand Luke—has a
company that makes terrific pretzels that are just the right size for these quick
and easy treats.

24 to 36 Newman's Own Pretzel Rods
(each 4 inches long) or 12 pretzel
logs (each about 8 inches long)

8 ounces premium dark chocolate,
chopped

Chill the pretzels in the refrigerator for 15 minutes. Create a prop to
support the pretzels in an upright position while the chocolate sets by
stacking 2 wire cooling racks, one on top of the other, so the parallel
wires are at a 90-degree angle to each other and form small squares
(If your wire cooling racks are already constructed with small squares,
then simply stack and align them one on top of the other.) Place the
racks on a sheet of parchment or waxed paper to catch any drips.

Place the chocolate in a medium heatproof bowl and set in a wide
pan or skillet of hot water. Set aside for 5 minutes, stirring 4 or 5 times,
and let it melt completely. Stir until smooth.

Pour the melted chocolate into a tall, narrow glass (I use an
inexpensive champagne flute). Dip each pretzel halfway into the
chocolate, then lift straight up and allow the extra chocolate to drip
back into the glass. Prop the dipped pretzel, chocolate end up, in one
of the wire "squares"; it will stand on its own at about a 45-degree
angle. Repeat with the remaining pretzels, making sure the chocolate

tips don't touch one another. Add more melted chocolate to the glass as the level decreases.

Let the chocolate set at room temperature, about 90 minutes. To serve, peel off any maverick chocolate that may have formed a drip. The pretzels are best enjoyed within 3 days and should be stored in layers, separated by parchment or waxed paper, in an airtight container at room temperature. (Since the dipping chocolate is not tempered, the coating will have a smooth, non-glossy surface. After several days, it will begin to mottle.)

VARIATIONS

For **Razzle-Dazzle Chocolate Pretzels**, follow the main recipe, setting aside toppings or coatings of your choice, such as turbinado sugar, colored sugar crystals, or chocolate sprinkles. After dipping and before propping, sprinkle the chocolate with your favorite topping. Proceed as directed.

Why not try chocolate potato chips too? For **Bet-You-Can't-Stop-at-One Chocolate Potato Chips**, follow the main recipe, substituting ruffle-style potato chips (I like Kettle's Krinkle Cut Sea Salt & Pepper) for the pretzels. Instead of pouring the chocolate into a tall glass, leave the chocolate in the bowl in which it was melted. Then, using a pastry brush, lightly brush a portion of the chip on both sides with chocolate.

CANDIES
and
NO-BAKE TREATS

a cluster of
TRUFFLES
makes about
30
TRUFFLES

A TRUFFLE MADE WITH FINE CHOCOLATE TASTES DIVINE.

It melts in your mouth, and the burst of chocolate flavor is nothing short of blissful. Classic ganache truffles are not difficult to make; you just need time. My favorite truffles are small, one-bite affairs, in which the cream is infused with the subtle flavor of an herb, spice, or tea. I also like them au naturel, unadorned except for a coating of cocoa powder.

GANACHE
½ cup heavy (whipping) cream
1 flavor infusion (options follows)
7 ounces premium dark chocolate, chopped
3 tablespoons unsalted butter, cut into pieces, at room temperature
Premium unsweetened cocoa powder for coating

FLAVOR INFUSIONS
(choose 1 of the following):
3 to 4 teaspoons chopped dried chipotle pepper
1 tablespoon peeled and finely chopped fresh ginger
Scant 1 teaspoon culinary lavender buds
1 teaspoon dried mint
1 premium Earl Grey tea bag such as Tazo, Taylors of Harrogate, or Twinings

In a small saucepan over medium-high heat, combine the cream and 1 flavor infusion, and heat until small bubbles appear around the edge of the pan. Remove from the heat, cover, and steep for 30 minutes. Using a fine-mesh sieve, strain out the flavoring, pressing to release any liquid. Discard the flavoring.

Rinse out the saucepan and return the cream to it. Reheat until small bubbles appear around the edges of the pan. Put the chocolate in a small heatproof bowl and pour the hot cream over it. Let stand for 3 minutes, then stir until smooth. Stir in the butter until blended. (If everything is not completely melted, place the bowl holding the chocolate mixture in a pan or wide skillet of hot water.)

In a shallow baking pan, spread the ganache into a layer about ¼ inch thick. After it reaches room temperature, cover with plastic wrap; let stand overnight at cool (60° to 70°F) room temperature. A finger pressed into the surface should leave a slight impression. (If the ganache is still too soft, you can place it very briefly in the refrigerator to chill it.)

Place the cocoa in a small, shallow bowl. Scoop up 1 teaspoon of ganache on a spoon or with a melon baller and gently shape into a ¾-inch ball about the size of a small hazelnut. Don't roll the ball too much; it's fine if the truffle is irregular. Drop the truffle into the cocoa and roll until lightly coated. (Wipe off your hands often with a dry towel for easier handling.) Transfer to a tray lined with parchment or waxed paper until all the truffles are coated. Store the truffles in airtight container at cool (60° to 70°F) room temperature for up to 3 days, or refrigerate for up to 2 weeks. Bring to room temperature before serving.

grown-up CHOCOLATE BUTTONS

makes
30
BUTTONS

HERE THE VERY BEST CHOCOLATE, A TASTE FOR DETAIL,

and a love of simplicity come together to create a delicious and sophisticated candy. Based on *mendiants*, a traditional French Christmas candy, these small and delicate coinlike chocolates are visually striking. While truffles may lure you with their size and bursts of chocolate flavor, these jewels will entice you with their beauty and purity of taste.

1 bar (3½ ounces) premium dark chocolate, chopped

About ½ ounce each of 2 or more of the following:
Candied citrus peel or crystallized ginger, slivered or diced
Dried fruit slivers such as golden raisins, cherries, apricots, or cranberries

Toasted pistachios, pecans, almonds, or peanuts, broken or slivered
Roasted and/or salted sunflower seeds
Spices such as freshly ground black pepper, nutmeg, sea salt, or chile powder blends
Finely ground espresso
Colored sugar sprinkles or turbinado sugar

Line a baking sheet with parchment paper. Draw thirty 1¼-inch circles, 6 per row. Turn the parchment over, pencil side down. Place the chocolate in a medium heatproof bowl in a wide pan or skillet of hot water. Set aside for 5 minutes, stirring 4 or 5 times, and let it melt completely. Stir until smooth.

continued

Using a teaspoon, fill each circle with about ½ teaspoon chocolate, doing 2 at a time. Allow the puddles to just set, then, using kitchen tweezers and the tip of a paring knife, artfully garnish each button with 1 or 2 toppings, pressing down lightly to make sure the garnishes stick. Allow the buttons to set in a cool place. Do not place them in the refrigerator, or they will discolor.

To serve, peel them off the parchment. Store the buttons in layers, separated by parchment or waxed paper, in an airtight container at a cool (60° to 70°F) room temperature. (Since the buttons are made without tempering the chocolate, they will have a smooth, non-glossy surface.) The buttons are best eaten within 3 days.

root-te-toot-toot CHOCOLATE FUDGE

makes
64
PIECES

SO, YOU'VE NOTICED THE FIRST INGREDIENT? BEFORE YOU
pass judgment, give this quirky fudge a try. It's easy, too, and the Raz-Ma-Taz
toppings are a kick. It's also a fun recipe to do with the kids. You'll find the fudge
is quite good. One thing is for sure: No one will guess the secret ingredient.

Using a small amount of Dutch-process cocoa powder gives the fudge a
dark color. If you don't have any, you can substitute regular cocoa.

²/₃ cup canned pinto beans (about
   4 ounces), drained and rinsed
1 cup premium unsweetened cocoa
   powder
½ cup (1 stick) unsalted butter, melted
2 tablespoons premium unsweetened
   Dutch-process cocoa powder

2 teaspoons pure vanilla extract
Up to 1 box (16 ounces) powdered
   sugar
1 cup chopped walnuts (optional)
Raz-Ma-Taz Sugar Blends for topping
   (pages 172-173)

Purée the beans or mash them through a sieve. Transfer the puréed
beans to a stand mixer and add the unsweetened cocoa, melted butter,
Dutch-process cocoa, and vanilla. On low speed, beat the mixture until
well blended. (Or, place all the ingredients except the powdered sugar
in the bowl of the mixer and puree with an immersion blender until
smooth.) Add the powdered sugar slowly at first to keep it from flying
around and continue to beat until the fudge reaches a thick and pliable
consistency. Beat in the walnuts, if desired.

continued

Outline an 8-by-8-inch square on a piece of parchment. Place the fudge in the center of the outlined square and, using clean hands, shape the fudge into a flat ¾-inch-thick square. Smooth the top with a rolling pin, and use a knife to clean and shape the edges. To cut the fudge into exact squares, first refrigerate it for 30 minutes. Then turn the chilled fudge over on a cutting board. Using a ruler and a paring knife, pointed straight down, cut the fudge into 1-inch pieces. Transfer each piece, bottom side up, to a plate. When you have cut all the fudge and the pieces have reached room temperature, frost by dipping the top of each piece into the sugar blends of your choice.

VARIATION

You could see this coming: **Roly-Poly Root-Te-Toot-Toot Chocolate Fudge.** Kids will love making these round candy treats, and the pliable candy also comes in handy as candleholders on "It's My Party" Birthday Cake (page 62). Follow the main recipe. Instead of forming the candy into an 8-inch square, form it into small trufflelike balls. Roll in powdered sugar or in a Raz-Ma-Taz Sugar Blend of your choosing.

RAZ-MA-TAZ SUGAR BLENDS

To make any of the following sugar blends, combine the ingredients in a small bowl and stir until well blended, or shake vigorously in a plastic container with a lid. (I use those nifty 4-ounce, resealable Ziploc or GladWare plastic containers.)

SALT AND PEPPER BLEND

¼ cup granulated sugar
½ teaspoon paprika
¼ teaspoon salt

⅛ teaspoon finely ground black pepper

CHILE AND COCOA BLEND

¼ cup demerara sugar

1 teaspoon chili powder

1 teaspoon premium unsweetened cocoa powder

CINNAMON AND PEPPER BLEND

¼ cup granulated sugar

1¼ teaspoons ground cinnamon

¼ teaspoon finely ground black pepper

CINNAMON AND COCOA BLEND

¼ cup granulated sugar

¾ teaspoon ground cinnamon

¾ teaspoon unsweetened cocoa powder

BARBECUE BLEND

¼ cup granulated sugar

1 teaspoon barbecue rub of your choice

SWEET CHILI BLEND

¼ cup granulated sugar

1 tablespoon chili powder

cacao-nib CRUNCH

makes about 2 CUPS

AT CACAO, IN DOWNTOWN PORTLAND, OREGON, OWNERS Aubrey Lindley and Jesse Manis are always finding new ways to use crushed cocoa beans or cacao nibs. These crunchy, sweet nuggets are, by far, my favorite. They are delicious as a snack, tossed in with your breakfast granola, or over an ice-cream sundae. Jesse even adds them to salads whenever chopped nuts are included.

1 cup superfine sugar
  (see Note, facing page)
½ cup water

1¾ cup premium cacao nibs, such as
  Scharffen Berger or Theo

This recipe depends on visual cues. The total cooking time is about 15 minutes.

Line a baking sheet with parchment paper or aluminum foil and set aside. In the bottom of a large, heavy-bottomed saucepan or Dutch oven with a pale interior, combine the sugar and water. Over medium-high heat, bring the mixture to a boil. Add the cacao nibs and stir a few times to coat them evenly in the sugar syrup, then let the mixture alone. As the syrup boils, it becomes thicker and big bubbles begin to form. When the moisture is almost gone, it will thicken and become sticky.

Begin stirring. The mixture will be quite sticky and then suddenly start to become sandy. When the sugar is completely sandy and has coated the nibs, remove the pan from the burner and continue to stir about 1 minute. Spread the nibs onto to the prepared baking sheet and cool completely. Store in an airtight container.

NOTE

Superfine sugar, also called baker's sugar, is available in supermarket baking sections. For a quick substitute, whirl 1 cup of granulated sugar at a time in a food processor or blender until fine, about 30 seconds.

crispy DARK CHOCOLATE EASTER EGGS

makes 12 2½-INCH EGGS

HERE'S TO THE KID IN EACH OF US—EVERYONE'S FAVORITE no-bake rice cereal treat wrapped in a great-tasting chocolate. Use the dark chocolate of your choice, and forget about hide-and-seek. Nestle the eggs in your Easter basket or serve them as a brunch delight on the prettiest plates you own.

8 ounces premium dark chocolate, chopped

3 tablespoons unsalted butter

20 large, fresh store-bought marshmallows (about 3 cups)

2 cups crispy rice cereal or crispy cocoa rice cereal

Decorative icing and candies (optional)

Coat an 8-by-8-inch baking pan with nonstick cooking spray. Line a baking sheet with parchment or waxed paper. Place the chocolate in a medium, heatproof bowl and set in a pan or wide skillet of hot water. Set aside for 5 minutes, stirring 4 or 5 times, and allow it to melt completely. Stir until smooth.

Meanwhile, in a large saucepan over low heat, melt the butter. Add the marshmallows and stir until completely melted, about 5 minutes. Turn off the heat, add the melted chocolate, and stir until blended. Pour the cereal over the chocolate mixture and fold in gently with a rubber spatula just until the cereal is coated.

Turn the mixture into the prepared pan and lightly press to evenly distribute. Let cool. To make each chocolate egg, firmly press a 2½-inch-long egg-shaped cookie cutter into the cereal mixture. Run your fingertips around the top perimeter of the cutter to make sure the cutter touches the bottom of the pan. Wriggle the filled cutter free, and slip the egg out of the cutter onto the parchment. Pat it back into shape if necessary. Repeat with the remaining cereal mixture. Any leftover cereal mixture is the cook's reward. If desired, decorate the eggs with icing and small candies. Store eggs in layers, separated by parchment or waxed paper, in an airtight container at a cool (60° to 70°F) room temperature. The eggs taste best if eaten within 3 days.

VARIATION

What could be better than two gifts in one, especially on Valentine's Day? For **Bittersweet Sweet Hearts**, follow the main recipe, using ten $2\frac{1}{4}$-inch-wide Valentine cookie cutters, one for each heart. After forming the heart, leave it in the cookie cutter and proceed as directed. Place each no-bake treat with its Valentine-shaped cookie cutter inside a small cellophane bag and secure with ribbon. After the chocolate heart is eaten, the cookie cutter can be used over and over again. To make your gift even sweeter, write out the recipe on individual cards and slip one into each gift bag so your friends can make their own.

bittersweet CARAMEL HONEYCOMB

makes about
1/2
POUND

YOU'LL FIND THIS SCRUMPTIOUS CANDY SURPRISINGLY
easy to make—and a little magical, too. It's the candy of my childhood. My
brother and I would get big chunks of it at the little blue store on the corner of
our street. Each piece was covered with dark or milk chocolate. I marveled at
all those wonderful, tiny holes. How did they get there?

Now I know. It happens when the baking soda comes in contact with the
hot sugar syrup. The mixture foams, creating spongelike holes that give the
candy its heavenly crunch once it's cooled. Be sure to follow the instructions,
word for word, and don't worry if you don't have a candy thermometer (I never
use mine for this recipe).

1½ teaspoons baking soda
1 cup granulated sugar
¼ cup water

3 tablespoons light corn syrup
4 ounces premium dark chocolate,
  melted (see page 23)

Lightly grease an 8-by-8-inch baking pan with cooking spray. To
remove the candy with ease, line the pan, lengthwise and widthwise,
with two 12-by-7-inch-wide sheets of parchment paper or aluminum
foil (shiny side up) and use the overhang as handles. (Since the paper
tends to fall inward towards the hot candy, you may want to use a
clothespin to secure the parchment on each edge.) Place the pan next
to where you will be cooking. In a small bowl, stir the baking soda to
get rid of any small lumps.

In a heavy, medium saucepan over medium-high heat, combine
the sugar, water, and corn syrup. Cook until the mixture becomes a

very pale straw color (300°F, hard-crack stage), swirling occasionally, about 10 minutes. Do not let the mixture get any darker. Remove from the heat and add the baking soda. The mixture will foam and expand.

Using a silicone spatula and working quickly, stir in the baking soda until it is blended and the color is even. Do not overwork. Pour the foaming syrup into the prepared pan. Do not spread, although you can tip the pan slightly to "move" the syrup a little toward each edge. Let set for 10 minutes. Pour the melted chocolate over the candy, tilting the pan to spread the chocolate over the surface. Let the candy rest at room temperature until it is set, about 3 hours. The cooler the room, the faster the chocolate will set. (You can speed up the process by placing the pan in the refrigerator for 10 minutes, but no longer.)

Once the candy is set, use the parchment or foil on both edges to lift from the pan. To cut into uniform pieces, turn the candy over. Using a metal ruler and a knife, score one length at a time, then bend. The candy will break along the score line. Continue in this fashion to cut the desired number of pieces. If you prefer, you can use the dull side of a heavy knife or cleaver to break the candy into bite-size pieces. Store in an airtight container at room temperature for up to 1 week.

VARIATION

To make **Caramel Crackers** to use as a garnish for other recipes in this book or as a treat all on its own, follow the main recipe, substituting a lightly oiled baking sheet for the baking pan. Pour the foaming syrup onto the prepared pan and let it spread. Do not coat with chocolate. Once the candy is set, use the dull side of a heavy knife or cleaver to break it into bite-size pieces.

SIP-IT OR SHAKE-IT
dark chocolate
DRINKS

HOT CHOCOLATE IN A HURRY
182

A QUARTET OF DRINKING CHOCOLATES
184

espresso float with dark chocolate ice cream and
vanilla-bean whipped cream
188

CLEAN-CHIC CHOCOLATE MARTINI
190

THE ITALIAN STALLION
191

HOT CHOCOLATE
IN A HURRY

Serves
1

WHETHER YOU HAVE FRIENDS FOR THE WEEKEND OR AN
after-school houseful of kids, there's no better treat than a rich cup of hot
chocolate for each and every one. Here's a recipe that lets you make one cup
or a team's worth in a hurry. After you prepare the rich chocolaty base, you
can refrigerate it for up to 10 days. When the mood strikes, making a cup is as
simple as scooping out 2 or 3 heaping tablespoons of the chocolate base and
stirring them into a mug of steaming milk.

6 ounces whole milk

2 to 3 heaping tablespoons Hot
Chocolate Base (facing page)

Miniature marshmallows or bakery-
style handmade marshmallows for
topping (optional)

In a small saucepan over medium heat, warm the milk until it is steaming, then pour it into a warmed mug. You can also warm the milk in a
mug in a microwave oven. Stir in the Hot Chocolate Base. You may like
the taste of it partially swirled or totally blended. Garnish with miniature marshmallows, if desired.

HOT CHOCOLATE BASE

makes

15 TO 20
SERVINGS

4 ounces premium unsweetened
  chocolate, chopped
½ cup water
⅔ cup granulated sugar

Pinch of salt
⅔ cup heavy (whipping) cream
½ teaspoon pure vanilla extract

In a heavy saucepan or in the top of a double boiler, combine the chocolate and water over low heat, whisking occasionally until smooth. (As the chocolate melts, it will appear stringy.) Add the sugar and salt and continue to cook and stir over low heat until the sugar dissolves, 3 to 4 minutes. Remove from the heat and let cool to room temperature.

In a stand mixer or with a hand mixer, whisk the cream and vanilla until stiff peaks form. Fold in the cooled chocolate mixture until blended. (Don't worry if tiny flecks of chocolate appear. They won't affect the delicious outcome.) Store in an airtight container in the refrigerator. The mixture will keep for up to 10 days.

VARIATIONS

For **Dark Chocolate Mocha**, follow the recipe for the Hot Chocolate Base. In a warmed 8-ounce mug, top 4 ounces of coffee or a double espresso with 1½ ounces brandy and 2 heaping tablespoons Hot Chocolate Base. Stir until partially or totally blended. Either way, the brew is delicious.

For **Hot Chocolate Brandied Eggnog**, follow the recipe for the Hot Chocolate Base. In a warmed 8-ounce mug, pour 6 ounces of warmed purchased eggnog. Top with 2 heaping tablespoons Hot Chocolate Base and a jigger of brandy. Mix. Stir until partially or totally blended. Garnish with a dusting of freshly grated nutmeg, if desired.

a quartet of
DRINKING
CHOCOLATES

each recipe yields between

2 8-OUNCE SERVINGS

AND **4** DEMITASSES

UNLIKE "HOT CHOCOLATE," DRINKING CHOCOLATES ARE deliciously thick and heady concoctions generally served in demitasse portions. They are adult drinks to linger over. Here are four very different examples.

As with all drinking chocolates, it is best to let the beverages rest for 10 minutes (or even overnight) before reheating briefly and serving. This pause gives the flavors and the velvety-smooth richness a chance to develop.

EUROPEAN-STYLE DRINKING CHOCOLATE

For lovers of European-style hot chocolate, serve unadorned or top with a dash of barely whipped cream or a grating of dark chocolate.

1 cup whole milk

½ cup heavy (whipping) cream

8 ounces premium dark chocolate, finely chopped

½ teaspoon cornstarch

1 to 2 teaspoons water

1 teaspoon pure vanilla extract

In a small saucepan over medium-low heat, heat the milk and cream until small bubbles form around the edges of the pan. Remove from the heat and stir in the chocolate until completely smooth. In a small bowl, dissolve the cornstarch in the water, then add to the chocolate mixture and stir until completely smooth and thick. Add the vanilla and stir until completely smooth. Let the hot chocolate rest, uncovered, for 10 minutes to develop its flavor and texture. Then briefly reheat over medium-low, while stirring constantly. Serve in warm cups.

CARAMEL DRINKING CHOCOLATE

My friend Jane says this is "a visit to grandmother in a cup." I say it's my next New Year's Eve eleventh-hour interlude, perhaps with a little brandy added. What's your vote?

1⅓ cups whole milk

3 ounces premium dark chocolate, finely chopped

6 tablespoons warm Caramel Sauce (page 159)

In a small saucepan over medium-low heat, heat the milk until small bubbles form around the edges of the pan. Remove from the heat and stir in the chocolate until completely smooth. Add the caramel sauce and stir until completely smooth. Let the hot chocolate rest, uncovered, for 10 minutes to develop its flavor and texture. Then briefly reheat over medium-low, while stirring constantly. Serve in warm cups.

SPICES OF ANTIQUITY DRINKING CHOCOLATE

Crushed cinnamon, whole cloves, and red pepper flakes give this drinking chocolate its spicy zest.

1½ cups whole milk

One 4-inch cinnamon stick, coarsely crushed with a meat tenderizer

4 whole cloves, crushed

Pinch to scant ¼ teaspoon red pepper flakes

3 ounces premium dark chocolate, finely chopped

¼ teaspoon pure vanilla extract

1 teaspoon firmly packed light or dark brown sugar (optional)

In a small saucepan over medium-low heat, heat the milk, cinnamon, cloves, and red pepper flakes until small bubbles form around the edges of the pan. Remove from the heat and let steep for 15 minutes. Strain the milk through a fine-mesh sieve and discard the spices.

continued

Rinse out the saucepan and return the milk to it. Reheat until small bubbles form around the edges of the pan. Remove from the heat and stir in the chocolate until completely smooth. Add the vanilla and brown sugar and stir until completely smooth. Let the hot chocolate rest, uncovered, for 10 minutes to develop its flavor and texture. Then briefly reheat over medium-low, while stirring constantly. Serve in warm cups.

TIME-TO-TARRY DRINKING CHOCOLATE

For an intriguing ending to a special meal, serve this sublime drinking chocolate in espresso cups. It is lighter in color than its three companions but I think it may be my favorite. With its subtle note of fresh tarragon, the drink takes on a surprisingly sophisticated taste.

½ cup heavy (whipping) cream
Twelve 6-inch sprigs fresh tarragon
Small pinch of salt

1 cup whole milk
3 ounces premium dark chocolate,
    finely chopped
Finely grated orange zest

In a small saucepan over medium-low heat, heat the cream, tarragon, and salt until small bubbles form around the edges of the pan. Remove from the heat, cover, and let steep at least 30 minutes or up to 2 hours. Strain the cream through a fine-mesh sieve and discard the tarragon.

Rinse out the saucepan and return the cream to it. Stir in the milk and heat until small bubbles form around the edges of the pan. Remove from the heat and stir in the chocolate until completely smooth. Let the hot chocolate rest, uncovered, for 10 minutes to develop its flavor and texture. Then briefly reheat over medium-low heat, while stirring constantly. Pour into warm cups. Add a pinch of orange zest to each cup and serve.

espresso float with
DARK CHOCOLATE ICE CREAM
and VANILLA-BEAN WHIPPED CREAM

serves
1

IF YOU HAVE AN ESPRESSO MACHINE OR COFFEE MAKER, this is one of the simplest and best chocolate coffee drinks you can make. Serve it in a glass, use a spoon to dip down and taste each layer, then hold the glass like a beverage and sip. The combination has everything. It's cool, creamy, hot, rich, deep, dark, and delicious.

2 scoops dark chocolate ice cream of your choice (my favorite is Deep, Dark Chocolate Ice Cream, page 134)

2 to 3 shots hot espresso

3 to 4 tablespoons Vanilla-Bean Whipped Cream (facing page) or Cacao-Nib Whipped Cream (page 77)

2 chocolate-coated espresso beans for garnish (optional)

Put the ice cream in an old fashioned or rocks glass. Pour the hot espresso over the ice cream. Top with the whipped cream, garnish with the espresso beans (if desired), and enjoy.

VANILLA-BEAN WHIPPED CREAM

1 cup heavy (whipping) cream

1 vanilla bean, split lengthwise and
  seeds scraped out

Pinch of salt

2 to 3 tablespoons granulated sugar

In a small saucepan over medium-high heat, combine the cream and
vanilla bean and seeds, and bring the mixture to a boil. Remove from
the heat, cover, and steep for 30 minutes. Taste to make sure it is
strongly flavored (when chilled, the flavor will be muted). Remove the
bean and refrigerate the cream, covered, for at least 4 hours or overnight. When ready to serve, whip the cream until it begins to thicken,
then add the salt and sugar. Continue beating until soft peaks form.
Refrigerate until ready to use.

clean-chic
CHOCOLATE
MARTINI

serves
1

WORK WAS DONE FOR THE WEEK, AND FRIDAY NIGHT
cocktail hour had arrived. "Let's have some fun," Debrah Vanchura said to her
husband, Joe. "Let's think up a chocolate martini." It sounded good to me, but
I wondered what they would use for an olive.

Debrah and Joe own Clean Chic, a state-of-the-art cleaning service in
Portland, Oregon. Debrah also owned a catering company for a number of
years, and she concocts great things in the kitchen. We owe this memorable
martini to her love of deep, dark chocolate.

Crushed ice

1 tablespoon powdered sugar

1 tablespoon unsweetened cocoa
   powder

1 lemon wedge

1 ounce vanilla-flavored vodka

1 ounce espresso or strong coffee

1 teaspoon granulated sugar

½ ounce chocolate liqueur

Dash of heavy (whipping) cream

Fill a martini glass and cocktail shaker or other lidded container with
crushed ice and let sit for 5 minutes to chill. Discard the ice. In a saucer,
mix the powdered sugar and cocoa until blended.

Run the lemon wedge around the rim of the glass. Dip and rotate
the rim in the powdered sugar mixture, making sure to keep the sugar
on the outside. Fill the shaker with more crushed ice. Add the vodka,
espresso, sugar, and chocolate liqueur. Cover and shake vigorously for
about 5 seconds. Strain the liquid into the glass. Drizzle a dash of heavy
cream into each glass and enjoy.

the ITALIAN STALLION

Serves 1

SLEEK, BOLD, AND A FAST RIDE TO FEELING GOOD.

Crushed ice
1¼ ounces Tuaca
¾ ounce Godiva chocolate liqueur

Dash of heavy (whipping) cream
Freshly grated nutmeg for sprinkling

Fill a martini glass and cocktail shaker or other lidded container with crushed ice and let sit for 5 minutes to chill. Discard the ice.

Fill the shaker with more crushed ice. Add the Tuaca and chocolate liqueur. Cover and shake vigorously for about 20 seconds. Strain the liquid into the glass. Float the heavy cream on top and sprinkle with nutmeg.

sources

DARK CHOCOLATE SOURCES

Here is a partial list of premium dark chocolates and their Web sites. Each site offers valuable information on chocolate as well as how and where to buy it. The first entry is an excellent Internet-only chocolate store for ordering a number of excellent dark chocolates.

CHOCOMAP:
www.chocomap.com
A great link to chocolate shops around the world.

CHOCOSPHERE, Portland, OR:
www.chocosphere.com

DAGOBA, Ashland, OR:
www.dagobachocolate.com

EL REY, Venezuela: www.chocolates-elrey.com

GREEN & BLACK'S, London, England:
www.greenandblacks.com

MICHEL CLUIZEL, Paris, France:
www.chocolatmichelcluizel-na.com

PRALUS, Roanne, France:
www.chocolats-pralus.com

SCHARFFEN BERGER, Berkeley, CA:
www.artisanconfection.com

THEO, Seattle, WA: www.theochocolate.com

VALRHONA, Paris, France: www.valrhona.com

BAKING SUPPLIES, INGREDIENTS, AND OTHER CHOCOLATE SUPPLIES

BOB'S RED MILL NATURAL FOODS
5209 S.E. International Way
Milwaukie, OR 97222
(800) 349-2173
www.bobsredmill.com

Nation's leader in stone milling, and offers a wide diversity of whole grains and natural foods, including shredded coconut.

KING ARTHUR FLOUR
The Baker's Catalogue
58 Billings Farm Road
White River Junction, VT 05001
(800) 827-6836
www.bakerscatalogue.com

Six types of cocoa, including black cocoa, as well as ingredients and equipment for the home baker are available from their online store.

PENZEYS, LIMITED, SPICES AND SEASONING
P.O. Box 933
Muskego, WI 53150
(800) 741-7787; (414) 574-0277
www.penzeys.com

A terrific selection of spices. Be sure to request a catalog (or download it). Great reading.

SCHARFFEN BERGER CHOCOLATE MAKER
914 Heinz Ave.
Berkeley, CA 94710
(800) 930-4528; (510) 981-4066
www.artisanconfection.com

Premium dark chocolates, cacao nibs, and natural cocoa powder. Their online store offers great value for bulk dark baking chocolate, natural cocoa powder, and cacao nibs. Smaller amounts are also available. This is the chocolate I used for testing the recipes in Deep Dark Chocolate.

SUR LA TABLE
184 Pine Street
Seattle, WA 98101
(800) 243-0852
www.surlatable.com

Assorted bakeware, cookware, pots, pans, and baking supplies, including premium dark chocolates.

WILLIAMS-SONOMA
P.O. Box 7456
San Francisco, CA 94120
(877) 812-6235
www.williams-sonoma.com

Assorted bakeware, cookware, pots, pans, and baking supplies, including imported chocolate.

WILTON INDUSTRIES, INC.
2240 West 75th Street
Woodridge, IL 60517
(800) 794-5866; (630) 963-1818
www.wilton.com

Assorted bakeware and baking and decorating supplies. Their online store carries the party cups that I use as stand-alone cupcake forms.

index

TABLE
of
EQUIVALENTS

The exact equivalents in the following tables have been rounded for convenience.

LIQUID/DRY MEASUREMENTS

U.S.	METRIC
¼ teaspoon	1.25 milliliters
½ teaspoon	2.5 milliliters
1 teaspoon	5 milliliters
1 tablespoon (3 teaspoons)	15 milliliters
1 fluid ounce (2 tablespoons)	30 milliliters
¼ cup	60 milliliters
⅓ cup	80 milliliters
½ cup	120 milliliters
1 cup	240 milliliters
1 pint (2 cups)	480 milliliters
1 quart (4 cups, 32 ounces)	960 milliliters
1 gallon (4 quarts)	3.84 liters
1 ounce (by weight)	28 grams
1 pound	448 grams
2.2 pounds	1 kilogram

OVEN TEMPERATURE

FAHRENHEIT	CELSIUS	GAS
250	120	½
275	140	1
300	150	2
325	160	3
350	180	4
375	190	5
400	200	6
425	220	7
450	230	8
475	240	9
500	260	10

LENGTHS

U.S.	METRIC
⅛ inch	3 millimeters
¼ inch	6 millimeters
½ inch	12 millimeters
1 inch	2.5 centimeters